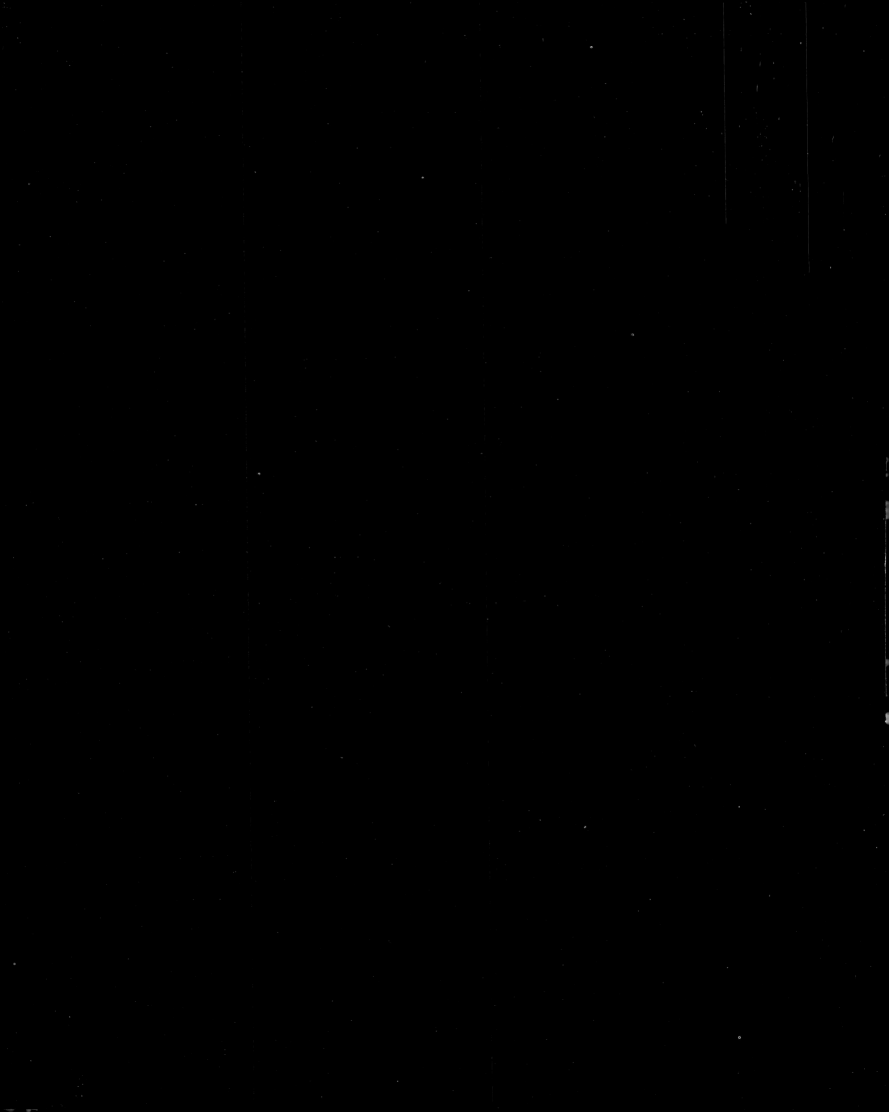

Previous page: National Commerce Bank in Jeddah, Saudi Arabia.
This page: Sunset over the skyscrapers of Chicago, Illinois.

SKYSCRAPERS

FORM & FUNCTION

SIMON & SCHUSTER
Rockefeller Center
1230 Avenue of the Americas
New York, New York 10020

A Marshall Edition
Conceived, edited, and designed by
Marshall Editions
170 Piccadilly
London W1V 9DD

Editor Heather Magrill
Art editor Eddie Poulton
Picture editor Richard Philpott

10 9 8 7 6 5 4 3 2 1

Library of Congress Cataloging-in-
Publication Data

Bennett, David, 1948-
    Skyscrapers : form & function / David
Bennett.
        p.   cm.
    ISBN 0-684-80318-6
    1. Skyscrapers—Design and construction.
    2. Skyscrapers—Case studies.   I. Title.
    TH1611.B46 1995
    720'.483—dc20   95-1018
                                              CIP

CONTENTS

FOREWORD

MUCH HAS BEEN WRITTEN ABOUT THE CREATION OF TOWERS, and many have searched for references that might show some deep spiritual reasoning to explain why the form has continued to reinvent itself down the centuries. The justifications of religion, defense, weather, expressions of power and ego have all been used to explain tall structures of every shape and form—from the earth mounds of prehistory, through the Mayan platforms and the pyramids of ancient Egypt, up to the most recent corporate skyscrapers.

I believe that the quest to go higher and higher, whether scaling mountains, creating earth-bound structures that will pierce the sky, or breaking free of gravity into flight, is a deep primal urge that can never be fully rationalized.

My partner, David Nelson, who has pioneered such ultra-high structures as the Millennium Tower—about twice the height of anything so far constructed—would probably not agree. He argues that the time has finally come for the rediscovery of the tower on the basis of necessity being the mother of invention. In a world with a burgeoning population, that is threatened also with global pollution, David believes increased density is the only way forward and that the skyscraper could be an ecological lifeline.

As humanists, we both agree that buildings are for people—to meet their needs, both material and spiritual—and quality of life can be the only measure of success. The technology involved is only a means to an end, never the end in itself—the goals must be social. This reinvention of the tower could, for the first time, really bring together a rich mixture of activities—living, working, and playing—in a vertical form. This new-age village could be the vertical high-density version of its historical rural model, with all the social benefits of proximity.

In a recent study for Shanghai, we were able to demonstrate that it is possible to build a mixed-use tower for 55,000 people that would be ecologically self-sufficient. It could accommodate the organic growth of the city without destroying any more valuable land—an immediate bonus would be a new park area—and would also be energy efficient—making no additional demands on the already overstretched power utilities. Part of its energy needs would be met through renewable sources, such as solar power, and more through reusing waste heat. This vertical village would also process and recycle its own trash, thereby minimizing strains on the existing infrastructure.

The ability of computers to help architects and engineers design ultra-high structures, as well as to model their environmental impact, has never been more advanced—the stage is set for a quantum leap!

Norman Foster

SIR NORMAN FOSTER

TALL STORIES

A DAY IN THE LIFE OF A SKYSCRAPER

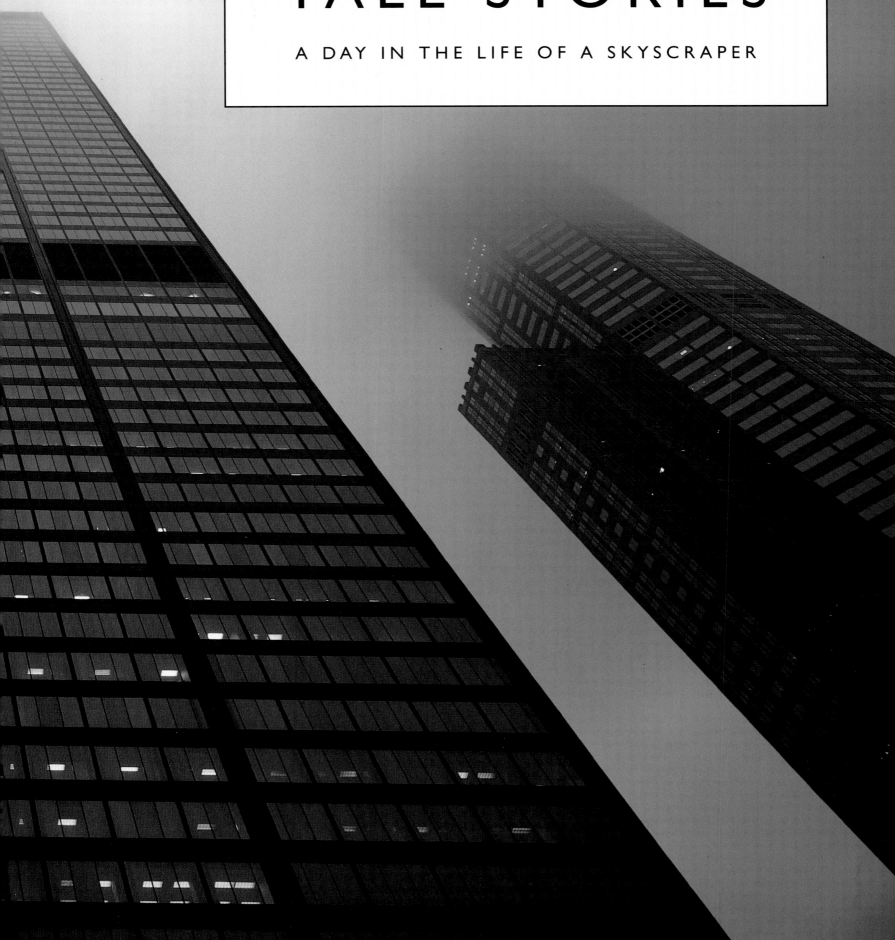

DAWN

No one can fail to be thrilled when they first see the Chicago skyline. The impact is immediate, dramatic, and exciting. It gives a feeling of pace, verve, and vitality. Chicago is also a city of extremes, not only in its ethnic origins and political culture, but also in its financial might and architectural style. It is known for gangland mobsters, flamboyant mayors, lifting bridges, blues music, and—fittingly for the city that was the cradle of the skyscraper—the tallest building in the world, the Sears Tower.

Perhaps it is the fact that it is the world's tallest building that fires the imagination when the silhouette of the Sears Tower looms on the horizon against the backdrop of the rising sun. Although it has much in common with other skyscrapers, this building also has a romance all of its own which only becomes apparent when the sheer scale and complexity of this "village in the sky" is understood.

The Tower rises above the city, the dawn sunlight warming its 16,100 bronze-tinted windows and 28 acres (11 ha) of black aluminum panels. Nothing moves except a small plume of steam coiling languidly around the broadcasting masts, which shows that the heat pumps and chillers, responsible for maintaining the shirt-sleeve environment inside the building, are working well.

Although the front doors are closed, and most of the building is in darkness, the Sears Tower never totally shuts down. Inside, security guards patrol the lobbies and corridors, checking that all is as it should be, and the last of the cleaners are polishing the travertine marble floors. The clearing up is complete, and the Tower is ready for the new day.

△ *Watched only by security cameras, a cleaner pushes his polishing machine across the travertine floor of the Calder lobby. By 4 A.M., the last patch of lobby floor has been polished. This job is left until last to prevent the floors from being scuffed before tenants arrive. At the back, the giant Calder Mobile, officially titled* Universe *and designed by sculptor Alexander Calder, continues its silent dance. It acts as a useful meeting point.*

EARLY MORNING

While most of Chicago sleeps, inside the Sears Tower a small band of people are hard at work. The busiest part of the building at this time of day is the loading bay on lower level 1. Each morning, between 6 A.M. and 8 A.M., 40 trucks arrive at the entrance on Lower Wacker Drive, 48 feet (15 m) below the main street level. Many of the trucks contain food for the restaurants; since this is perishable, it must be unloaded immediately and transferred to the cold rooms of the Levy restaurant chain. Here people are also busy with preparations for the food delivery service, Chef's Express, which opens at 5:30 A.M.; and for Caffè Tazza and Mrs. Levy's Delicatessen which start serving food at 6 and 6:30 A.M. respectively.

The rest of the vehicles in the loading bay contain general deliveries to the building, such as cleaning and office supplies, stationery, and, most importantly, mail. Once unloaded, the letters and packages are taken to the mail room, which is part of the post office, also on lower level 1, where a group of clerks

"The consolation of the night shift is that a lot of the problems of the day are behind you"

begins to divide it up by floor and company. By 8:30 A.M. the mail is ready for collection by the tenants.

Although a number of people have worked in the Sears Tower since it opened in 1974, no one knows its history better than Phil Chinn, the general manager of the building for 10 years and now the tenant representative. He even worked, on behalf of the Sears, Roebuck corporation, on the initial designs for the Tower when they were first discussed with the principal architects, Fazlur Khan and Bruce Graham of Skidmore, Owings & Merrill. "Richard Sears worked for the Minneapolis and St. Louis Railroad and sold watches in his spare time by placing ads in magazines and local papers. In 1886 he started to sell them by mail order and a year later, when business was booming, he employed Alvah Roebuck to repair the faulty watches that were being returned.

"Seven years later, in 1893, Sears and Roebuck became partners and moved the newly established Sears, Roebuck and

◁ *Inside the command center, much of the available wall space is covered with screens that provide constantly updated information for the duty officers about the status of the building.*

For example, one set of screens monitors all the equipment that keeps the building functioning properly. The computers will alert the duty engineer to any change in the status of a piece of machinery so that problems that arise can be dealt with promptly.

Another bank of screens shows the output from dozens of remote-controlled cameras, strategically concealed in all the public areas of the building. The screens allow the duty security officer to keep an eye on everything that is happening and direct his security officers to areas in which they might be needed. If there is an incident, the cameras can be zoomed in to pick up the smallest detail—even something as tiny as the face of Washington on a dime dropped on the floor. Every piece of important information is recorded, logged, and filed.

◁ *In the loading bay, several trucks are being unloaded. The vehicle partially hidden behind the pillar on the left is carrying refrigerated food for the Levy restaurant chain, while next to it is a large Express Mail truck. More than 40 trucks enter the loading bay early each morning.*

Company to Chicago, where it has remained ever since. Within a decade their company had become the biggest mail-order business in Chicago, making millions of dollars and employing hundreds of local people."

By the 1960s, Sears, Roebuck was one of the most important trading companies in the United States and the largest mail-order business in the world. But its merchandising operations and 12,000 employees were scattered across Chicago in 17 different buildings. The chairman, Gordon Metcalf, decided it was time to centralize the business and acquired a site for a new building. It had to be large enough to provide the 2.5 million square feet (230,000 m²) of floor space the company needed at the time and have a further 1 million square feet (93,000 m²) for the expansion that was expected through to the year 2000. The resulting 110-story Sears Tower, completed in 1974, was the world's tallest building.

Up in the command center it is 6 A.M., and a bank of monitors shows empty corridors and lobbies; the monotony is broken only by an occasional guard. Another set of screens displays the status of the building's equipment. Computers constantly check the amount and temperature of

△ *The "midnight army" is glad to be at the end of a night spent refitting offices on the 43rd floor. Contractors must use the freight elevators to move around the building rather than the more stylish tenant elevators.*

the air entering and leaving the "lungs" of the Tower, the chiller units on the 29th floor, as well as the electricity being consumed by the building. Other screens give a floor-by-floor reading of the air temperature and the lights that are still on. From all this information, the duty engineer can see that the entire system is functioning correctly, a fact that is confirmed by the reassuring throb coming up through the floor from the machines of the central plant rooms.

"The consolation of the night shift is that a lot of the problems of the day are behind you," reflects Randy, one of the four duty engineers coming to the end of his shift in the command center. There are relatively few people to keep track of, since much of the building is completely empty. This is the time of day for routine maintenance checks and essential repairs.

Each night, a team of six building engineers, assisted by outside contractors, carry out any maintenance that is necessary. During their shift, they may replace parts on a chiller, inspect the elevators, change a fluorescent tube in one of the 145,000 lights, or even fix a plumbing leak in one of the 796 taps in the washrooms.

MORNING

The morning rush hour in downtown Chicago begins at about 7:30 A.M. By 8:30 A.M. the trickle of people arriving at the entrances on Franklin Street and South Wacker Drive has become a flood. For the 10,000 people who work in the Sears Tower each day, its location is ideal. Being at the western end of "The Loop," Chicago's financial district, it is close to train and bus terminals and to three expressways.

Inside the building, the elevator system is designed to get people to their floors as efficiently as possible. It does this using a total of 104 elevators. Eight are for freight, two serve the Skydeck, and the rest are for tenants. Those who work above the 34th floor must use one of the 28 double-decker elevators, traveling at 1,600 feet (490 m) per minute, which whisk people straight up to the sky-lobbies at levels 33–34 and 66–67. These skylobbies are two-story interchange points, with escalators to connect the two floors. They give access to the single-decker elevators, of which there are 66, that take people to individual floors. Although the system seems complex, it is well marked and tenants soon get used to it.

By 8 A.M. Margaret Lamason, the facilities manager for Cargill Investor Services, has had her morning workout and is at her desk on the 23rd floor. One of her first jobs is to send an assistant down to the mail room on lower level 1 to collect the day's mail. Courier packages are both received and dispatched from a kiosk on the Franklin Street side of the building.

While a customer sips a cup of coffee in Caffè Tazza on the concourse, the kitchens of the Levy restaurant group are a hive of activity. Since this chain runs all of the food outlets except Burger King on lower level 1 and the Metro-politan Club on the 67th floor, all food deliveries are stored and sorted in a central "pantry." Around 8:30 A.M., Giorno, chef of the Mia Torre restaurant, checks the food before it is sent up from the pantry and supervises his five cooks as they prepare the lunches.

Meanwhile on Franklin Street, John Simpson, president of Hill, Steadman and Simpson, a law firm on the 85th floor, slips his car into one of the 149 spaces in the basement garage. For this privilege, he pays $400 a month excluding valeting.

▷ *People arriving at the Wacker Drive entrance push through one of three revolving doors into the four-story atrium. From there, they walk down a short flight of marble steps into the main Calder lobby. Any tourists entering the atrium by mistake are met by a security guard and redirected out of the Tower and around to the Skydeck pavilion.*

△ *On the 44th floor, senior executives of the John Buck Company, the managing agents of the Sears Tower, have a breakfast meeting with the tenant representative Phil Chinn (seated second from the left) to discuss lease agreeements. Even from this relatively low floor, there are fabulous views.*

△ *A workout before work is possible at the Sears Tower Health Club on lower level 3. It opens at 6 A.M. and offers those who work in the Tower either an exercise class or an individual workout.*

As the sun rises higher in the sky, the aluminum and glass on the outside of the steel-framed Tower start to expand, giving an occasional creak and groan. Whatever the weather outside—whether snow is lying on the streets, or Chicago is suffering in a heatwave—the temperature inside is always pleasant.

The Sears Tower is a colossal 1,454-foot (443-m) high airtight container, sealed from the outside world by a glass skin and held together by 76,000 tons of steel. The comfortable atmosphere inside is maintained by an air-handling system which consists of a network of aluminum ducts running in the ceiling spaces. These ducts act like arteries and veins transporting freshly filtered air, of the right temperature and humidity, around the building and removing stale air.

During the day, there is an inevitable buildup of heat from the thousands of computers and copiers, the body heat of the

people, and the sun streaming in through the windows. Any change in air temperature is picked up by electronic sensors and relayed to the command center. There, the duty engineer can adjust the output of the chillers and thus control the quality and amount of air flow around the building.

By mid-morning, the 10,000 people who make up the daytime population of the Sears Tower are hard at work in their offices, which range from those of law or accountancy firms to investment brokers or engineering consultants. The support staff, in the restaurants, bank, and hair salon to mention but a few, are also into their routines. By this time, there is also a steady flow of tourists visiting the Skydeck on the 103rd floor. To allow the building to function effectively both as a place of work and as a tourist attraction, a separate tourist entrance—the Skydeck pavilion—was built on Jackson Boulevard.

◁ **On a clear day** it is possible to see four states (Illinois, Michigan, Wisconsin, and Indiana) from the 1,353-foot (412-m) high Skydeck, the observation floor of the Sears Tower.

On an average day, some 5,000 tourists enter the Skydeck pavilion (far left) on Jackson Boulevard. From this entrance, they take a short elevator ride down to lower level 2, buy a ticket, and are then ushered into the "Chicago Experience." This is a slide show followed by an exhibition, the highlight of which is a 9-foot (2.7-m) tall model of the Tower itself. Here the 1.5 million people who visit the Skydeck each year discover that the Sears Tower contains enough concrete to build a 5-mile (8-km) long, eight-lane wide highway and enough steel to make 52,000 cars.

From here, people take one of the two elevators up to the Skydeck on the 103rd floor (left). Using the leaflet provided, which details exactly 199 points of interest, the tourists slowly work their way around the Tower trying to identify as many features as possible. For a closer look at the breathtaking view, there are powerful binoculars mounted on all sides of the Skydeck.

▷ **The most unusual visitors** to the Sears Tower must be the falcons, which use the corner setbacks at levels 66 and 90 as vantage points when searching for prey. Although they nest on a building on the other side of the road, about level with the 33rd floor, the birds take advantage of the updrafts produced by the Sears Tower to reach their hunting perches as effortlessly as if they were taking an elevator ride. And once they have made a catch, usually a small bird or pigeon but occasionally a woodpecker, they often return to the same spot to feast—a distracting sight for some people on the other side of the glass.

"The falcons were introduced into the city to help control the pigeon population. It is impressive to see them from the windows of the higher floors gliding by or just hovering on the thermals on a hot day."
Tom Cronin, chief engineer.

LATE MORNING

Alarm bells ring in the command center when anemometers on the roof detect wind speeds of more than 40 mph (65 km/h). Problems only occur when the wind rises to a speed of 60 mph (100 km/h). Although this only makes the top of the building sway by less than a foot (30 cm), barely perceptible inside the Tower, even such a small movement could be enough to jam the Skydeck and freight elevators—those with the longest cables, suspended from cable drums on the 106th floor. To avoid any problems, and the unwelcome prospect of a 2,232-step climb down from the Skydeck to the lobby, the speed of these elevators is reduced and, to correct any sway, they are stopped for a moment at every 10th floor. Since the local elevators cover only relatively short distances, their operating speeds are usually just reduced.

It is 11 A.M. and on lower level 1 a lawyer from the 58th floor is having his teeth checked by Alan Moses, the dentist. Without stepping outside the building, people can get smartened up from top to toe. On the same level, in A Cut Above, Karen Kennedy and her eight stylists keep clients' hair beautiful, while on lower level 2, Sam, the Shoe Doctor, shines their shoes. Meanwhile, on the ground floor, the last of the

▷ *Six wash robots, each weighing 2 tons, clean the outside of the building eight times a year. The washing component is lowered down the building on cables at a rate of 45 feet (14 m) per minute. It squirts sud-free detergent onto the windows and then brushes, rinses, and vacuums it off, all in one movement. The dirty water is then filtered by the unit and recycled.*

▽ *Twin aerials, or masts, each measuring 253 feet (77 m) were added to the Tower in 1983, taking its height to 1,707 feet (520 m) at the tips. The welded steel tube structures, which resemble the barrel of a giant gun when seen from inside, are used by 21 broadcasting stations.*

food outlets, including Eadie's Kitchen and Market, and the Mia Torre and Dos Hermanos restaurants, have opened for business.

In his office on the 31st floor, the chief engineer, Tom Cronin, his top pocket bulging with a digital thermometer, 6-inch (15-cm) ruler, pen, screwdriver, allen key, pocket calculator, and thermostatic probe, has returned from his morning inspection. "I find quite a few small birds and bats stunned or dead on the roof at level 66, but not anywhere else. They probably mistake the glass for clear air or are caught up in the swirling updrafts and fly straight into the building."

In addition to clearing dead creatures from the roofs, he and his staff of 27 engineers are responsible for maintaining the 16,100 panes of external glass, 22,000 tons of machinery, 104 elevators, 18 escalators, 145,000 light fixtures and other electrical installations, 25,000 miles (40,000 km) of plumbing, 6 wash robots, and even the heated sidewalks that melt away ice and snow from around the building in winter.

Tom Cronin is very pleased with the performance of the Tower during its biggest trial, the Great Flood of 13 April 1992. The worst disaster to hit Chicago since the fire of 1871, it shut the city down for weeks. A wooden pile being driven for a jetty breached an old network of coal tunnels, which soon filled with water and ended up flooding the basements of hundreds of buildings. Thanks to the diaphragm wall that enclosed the basement, the Sears Tower remained completely dry, although it too had to be evacuated because of the danger from other buildings and the loss of vital city services.

▽ **In the Metropolitan Club**, *a private dining club on the 67th floor, Jacques Coutelle, the manager, and Joe O'Donnell, the chef, put the finishing touches on the lunch buffet. Around 2,000 members of the business community pay to enjoy the amenities of this exclusive club, with its complimentary breakfast and gourmet lunches and dinners.*

LUNCHTIME

At some time between midday and 3 P.M., people in the Sears Tower go to lunch. Suddenly, the corridors, escalators, elevators, skylobbies, and transfer floors are full of tenants. Since this is the busiest time of the day for the restaurants, it is necessary to reserve a table to enjoy the Mexican food served at Dos Hermanos or the Italian menu at Mia Torre. However, if these places are full, there are always the less expensive food outlets, including Eadie's Plaza Cafe and Mrs. Levy's Delicatessen, where the Herman Muenster—fresh bread topped with scrambled eggs, muenster cheese, and broiled sausages—is highly recommended.

If even these places are full and the weather is sunny, it can make a pleasant change to eat alfresco on the Plaza. Some people bring their own food, while others buy a stuffed potato from Eadie's Kitchen and Market or a sandwich and refreshing lemonade from Caffè Tazza. In fact, in the summer, eating outside is one of the most popular options, especially since most of the restaurants and food kitchens offer a take-out service. And for those who have to work through lunch, there is always the Chef's Express which can deliver a delicious three-course meal straight to the boardroom.

For most, the search for food takes them down to the lobby, but for some, the members of the exclusive Metropolitan Club, it takes them to the 67th floor. Here the $10 lunch buffet is already busy, and Jacques Coutelle, the manager, is always on hand to welcome members and their guests to the stunning views and sumptuous delights of one of the finest eating houses in Chicago.

To join this club, business people must be sponsored by an existing member, be approved by the club committee, pay a one-off fee of $1,000, and an additional monthly fee of $100 on top of what they eat and drink. In addition to the daily meals, the club also holds regular cigar and port evenings, and has a dinner-dance every Saturday night.

John Simpson, president of Hill, Steadman and Simpson, a law firm on the 85th floor, is a frequent visitor: "I am one of the founder members of the Metropolitan Club and also one of the first tenants in the

△ **Chef Giorno (above), stands behind his colorful creation, the "Insalata Bar," just one of the gastronomic delights that tempt people into the Mia Torre restaurant for lunch. The doors open at 11 A.M., and by noon it is usually full. The welcoming decor of this Italian-style eating house is based on summer in Siena and the warm colors of the Mediterranean.**

◁ **Just an elevator ride away from the office, down on lower level 1, is Karen Kennedy's hair salon A Cut Above. Here, between 8:30 and 5:30, a wash, cut, and blow dry can be had in just 30 minutes from one of the eight stylists. Favorite customers are seen by Karen herself. And all of this is possible without having to brave the potentially disastrous effects of the wind or rain outside on the way back to the office.**

Sears—we moved in back in 1974. I always eat there, take the buffet at lunch, take clients there for dinner. Without doubt it is the best restaurant-cum-dining club in Chicago. Superb food, excellent service…one of the great assets of the building."

During the day, the building is patrolled by around 40 uniformed security personnel. Some of them work in the basements and garage area, most are assigned to look after the public areas of the building itself, and a few stay in the command center, constantly scanning the surveillance screens. Rick Griffin, the director of security, is proud of his team and the work that they do. "We try to be visible at all times. We check unattended packages, the comings and goings of people, and the well-being of the building 24 hours a day. We are trained in first aid, in cardiovascular resuscitation, and in handling firearms. You won't find that kind of protection in your own home."

After lunch, many people take the opportunity to do a few errands. On the ground floor, people file into the Old Kent Bank. Some use the automatic cash dispensers while others join the line for the bank tellers. Although the lines are longest at lunchtime, they are far better than in the days before there was a cash dispensing machine; then you could stand in line for 20 minutes just to cash a check. Elsewhere in the Tower, people take the opportunity to use the post office, get their shoes cleaned, their hair done, their teeth checked, or just to browse on the newsstand on the ground floor.

▷ *Tenants can cash a check or draw money from a cash dispenser at the Old Kent Bank without leaving the building, since it has two entrances, one inside the Tower and another on South Wacker Drive. In the days when the Sears, Roebuck corporation occupied much of the building, the bank was located on the third floor and looked after the money of thousands of employees and tenants.*

In 1988, Sears, Roebuck left the building, and the John Buck Company became the building managers. To attract new tenants, the Sears Tower was comprehensively redeveloped by architects DeStefano and Partners. Part of this package included relocating the bank to the ground floor.

EARLY AFTERNOON

At times, the noise on the streets of Chicago is deafening, but cocooned behind a wall of glass and steel, the working community of the Sears Tower is oblivious to it all. Those in the upper floors, however, soon become aware of other sounds as the building moves in the wind. Looking out of the window of his 77th-floor office, John Lynch, a senior partner with the law firm Latham & Watkins, confesses to being scared at times.

"On very windy days, the building sways noticeably and I sometimes have to spread my feet a little to steady myself against the movement. Sometimes the corner columns creak and groan like a wooden galleon, and my window pane flaps and vibrates so alarmingly that I abandon my office suite and work behind a walled partition, away from the glass."

He can remember the time that it rained glass—debris from a nearby building that was under construction smashed into some of the glass panels. But in 20 years, John Lynch cannot remember an elevator breaking down, the power failing, the lights blacking out, or an occasion when he or any of his staff ever shivered from cold or sweltered in the heat.

"On very windy days, the building sways...the corner columns creak and groan...and my window pane flaps and vibrates so alarmingly that I abandon my office"

A man in white overalls is suspended in a cradle from the 109th floor. He is inspecting the building's 76,000-ton steel frame, the sealing around the windows, and the integrity of the plastic film over the glass. Every year, the entire curtain wall is thoroughly checked. This inspection is part of a systematic maintenance program, rigorously followed to mend and replace components before they fail. In the early years, there were many cases of breaking glass which led to bad press, but this has all been sorted out.

In front of the Calder Mobile, a group of visitors listens to Drew Neiman's sales pitch. As leasing director for the managing agents, the John Buck Company, he is responsible for filling any empty tenant space. He tells them about the redevelopment of the building after the Sears, Roebuck corporation moved out in 1988. A finance package was put together, and the John Buck Company was appointed to redevelop the site and so improve its leasing potential and profitability. Architects DeStefano and Partners were employed to design the Skydeck entrance, to keep the tourist and business functions of the building separate, and to remodel the public areas.

◁ *Refurbishing office space is carried out both day and night. New partitions, ceilings, and light fixtures are installed, and the space is decorated in the colors and finishes chosen by the new tenant. Since the redevelopment of the Sears Tower, the renting of space has been a success story. Even the huge floors between 37 and 50, traditionally the hardest to rent, are starting to attract tenants.*

Running parallel to the window are two of the large 3-foot (0.9-m) deep trusses that support the floor above. These 75-foot (23-m) long trusses have been boxed in, but, where the ceiling has been stripped away above the contractor, part of a smaller intermediate floor brace can be seen.

▽ *The 29th floor is home to the chillers* that control the temperature of the air that is pumped around the building. There are five chillers—three weighing 5,000 tons and two of 1,800 tons each—which are effectively huge refrigerators for cooling water. Air is pushed through the water to chill it and then pumped to the five plant zones (on lower levels 2–3 and on levels 29–32, 64–65, 88–89, and 104–109). From there, it goes to the individual floors. The chillers are monitored on computer screens in the chiller plant room and command center, and progress reports can be printed out (right).

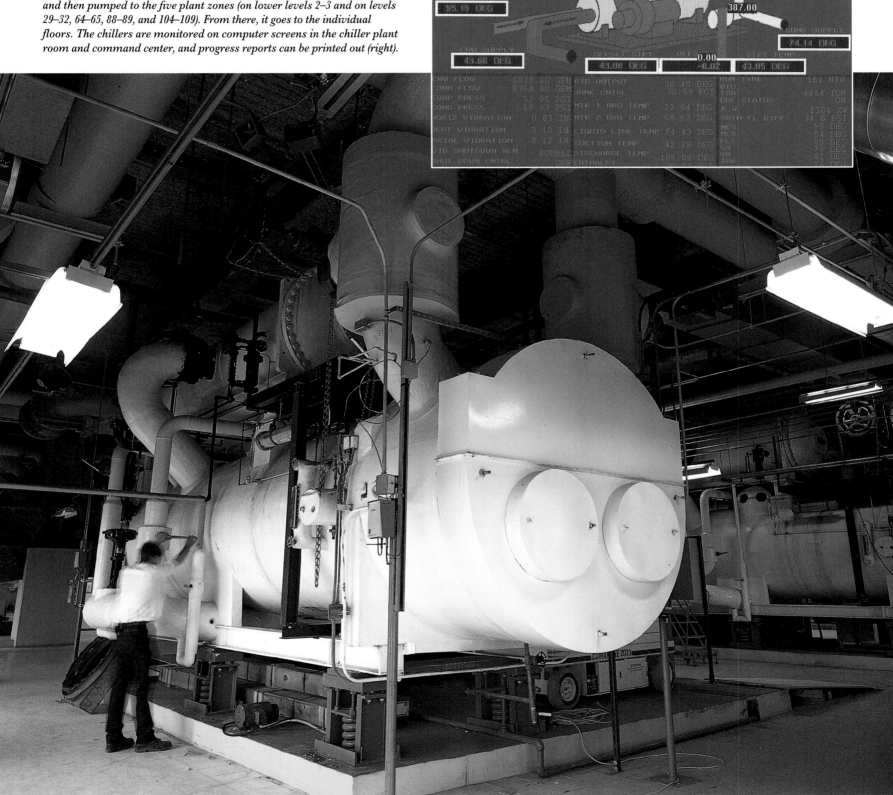

THE SEARS TOWER

Designed to accommodate around 10,000 employees of Sears, Roebuck and Company, as well as 6,000 other tenants, the Sears Tower became the world's tallest building when it was completed in 1974. It rises 1,454 feet (443 m) to the roof, the point to which all the official measurements are taken, and a further 253 feet (77 m) to the tips of the aerials.

Although the Sears Tower is 204 feet (62 m) taller than the Empire State Building, it actually weighs far less—223,000 tons against 365,000 tons. It is one of the most innovative mega-structures of all time and was designed by Fazlur Khan of Skidmore, Owings & Merrill, one of the great pioneers of supertall structures. The structure, known as a bundled tube, consists of a bundle of nine tubes—each one a rigid steel frame of columns and beams measuring 75 feet (23 m) on each side—which are interconnected along their common sides. Overall, the Sears Tower is, therefore, three tubes long on each side. The steel frame weighs just 76,000 tons and supports a floor area of 3.7 million square feet (344,000 m²), equivalent to about 65 football fields.

All nine tubes rise together for the first 49 floors, where two of the corner tubes terminate. The remaining seven climb to the 65th floor, where the other two corner tubes stop. The remaining five sections rise with a cruciform plan to the 89th floor, where three more tubes are cut off, leaving just two to reach the 109th floor. A small penthouse on the roof houses the cooling towers and the uppermost wash robot.

Calder lobby

People arriving at the Wacker Drive entrance to the Sears Tower move through the arched atrium and down some stairs into the Calder lobby. This four-story space is dominated by *Universe*, a moving mural, measuring 55 feet (17 m) wide by 33 feet (10 m) high, which was designed by the renowned American sculptor Alexander Calder.

The Calder lobby is overlooked on two sides by the mezzanine on level 3. Before the redevelopment of the building, the lobby and mezzanine were used by both business people and tourists and included souvenir shops, boutiques, and restaurants.

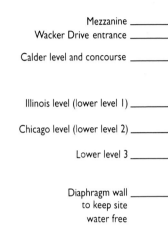

Mezzanine _____
Wacker Drive entrance _____
Calder level and concourse _____

Illinois level (lower level 1) _____
Chicago level (lower level 2) _____
Lower level 3 _____

Diaphragm wall to keep site water free

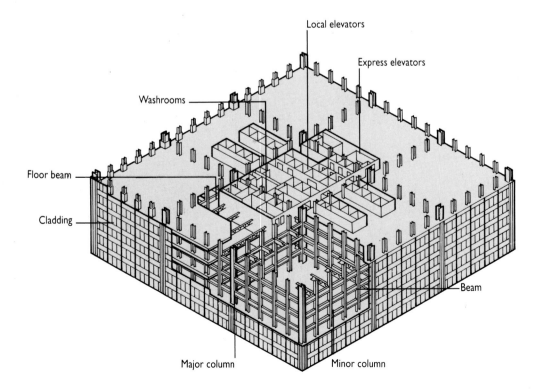

Local elevators

Express elevators

Washrooms

Floor beam

Cladding

Beam

Major column

Minor column

The basics of the bundled tube

Up to the 49th floor, all nine tubes of the structure rise together. The outside of each tube is made up of a row of sixteen 40-inch (1-m) wide steel columns, with their centers 15 feet (4.6 m) apart. The columns are braced by 42-inch (1.1-m) deep beams at each floor level. With all of the supporting steel on the outside, the interior of each tube, measuring 75 feet (23 m) on each side, is free of columns.

Each level is bridged by a series of 3-foot (0.9-m) deep trusses, or floor beams, which support the metal deck onto which the concrete floor is poured. The washrooms, local plant rooms, and banks of elevators are all clustered around the center of each floor, leaving the more desirable window areas free for offices. And the whole building is enclosed by a curtain wall of 16,100 bronze-tinted reflective windows and 28 acres (11 ha) of black-coated aluminum panels.

Aerials

The 253-foot (77-m) tall aerials are clustered with signal transmitters, receivers, and boosters. The Sears Tower is home to 21 networks which use these antennae, together with the aerials on the roof of one of the setbacks at level 90, to broadcast to the surrounding area. The white, missile-shaped masts are protected from lightning strikes by a metal earthing cable that runs right down to the ground.

Cooling towers

Four large cooling towers, each 24 foot (7 m) square and nearly three stories high, are located on levels 106–109. Each tower, two of which can be seen here, has metal walls with fins and a large central fan. Water that has already been used in the chillers is pumped to the top of each tower, then, as it cascades down the inside walls, it is cooled by the draft from the fan.

Skydeck

The observation deck on the 103rd floor is 1,353 feet (412 m) above street level, and on a clear day, with the horizon as much as 50 miles (80 km) away, it is possible to see the four states of Illinois, Indiana, Michigan, and Wisconsin. Visitors to the Skydeck are able to listen to as many as seven different prerecorded messages, each of which points out the various features that can be seen by day and by night.

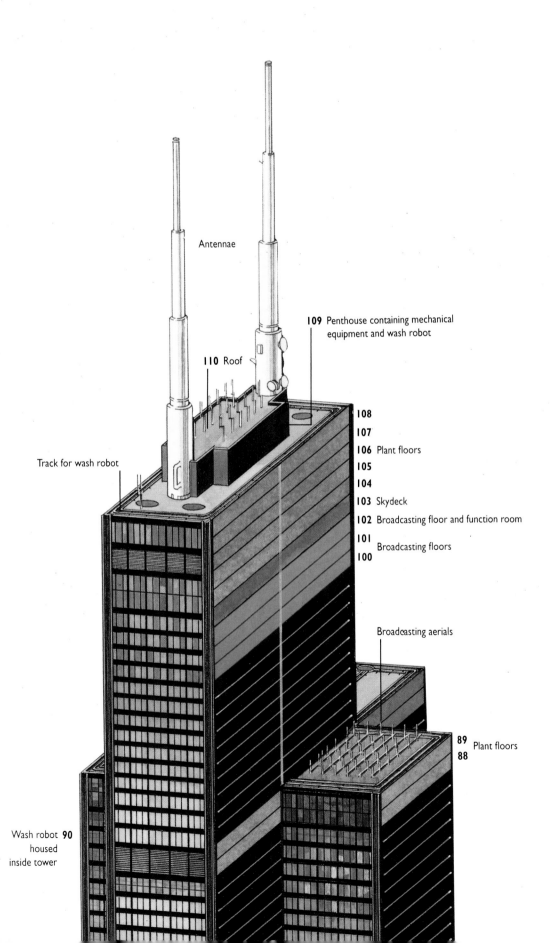

Antennae

109 Penthouse containing mechanical equipment and wash robot

110 Roof

Track for wash robot

108
107
106 Plant floors
105
104
103 Skydeck
102 Broadcasting floor and function room
101
100 Broadcasting floors

Broadcasting aerials

89 Plant floors
88

Wash robot **90** housed inside tower

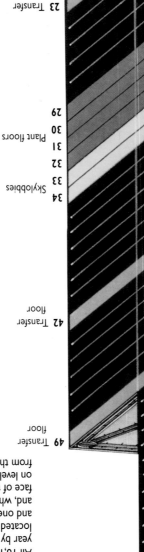

Plant floors

Most of the machinery that keeps the Tower running smoothly is housed at five points up the building—on lower levels 2–3 and levels 29–32, 64–65, 88–89, and 104–109—although each floor has some local plant, such as air-handling boosters. The major plant floors contain electrical substations, water and air-handling machinery and elevator hoist motors (above).

Skylobbies and transfer floors

Double-decker express elevators speed people nonstop from the concourse to the skylobbies at levels 33–34 and 66–67. These skylobbies are two-story concourses, linked by escalators, leading to banks of single-decker elevators, which travel to intermediate floors. Since each bank of elevators only serves a small group of floors, people can change between local elevators at transfer floors.

Wash robots

All 16,100 of the Tower's windows are cleaned eight times a year by one of six wash robots. The robots are permanently located on roof setbacks, two at level 50, two at 66, one at 90, and one at 109. They move around the edge of the roof on rails and, when in position, lower the washing mechanism down the face of the building on cables. On some faces, the wash robot on level 109 must drop its washing mechanism 1,405 feet (438 m) from the roof to clean the windows just above street level.

10 Transfer floor

17 Transfer floor

23 Transfer floor

29
30 Plant floors
31
32
33 Skylobbies
34

42 Transfer floor

49 Transfer floor

Housing for wash robot

Metropolitan 67 Club

64 Plant floors
65
66 Skylobbies
67

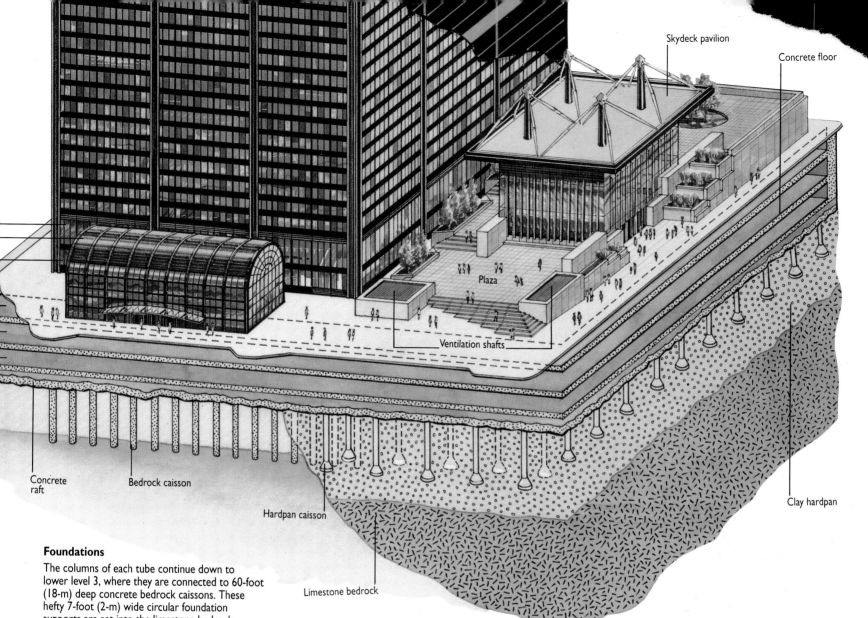

Skydeck pavilion

Concrete floor

Plaza

Ventilation shafts

Concrete raft

Bedrock caisson

Hardpan caisson

Limestone bedrock

Clay hardpan

Foundations

The columns of each tube continue down to lower level 3, where they are connected to 60-foot (18-m) deep concrete bedrock caissons. These hefty 7-foot (2-m) wide circular foundation supports are set into the limestone bedrock to anchor the whole structure.

Since bedrock caissons are only necessary under the Tower, the rest of the site is supported by 3-foot (0.9-m) wide hardpan caissons which extend just 22 feet (6.7 m) into the clay hardpan. The foundations are all connected to a massive concrete raft which also forms the lowest basement floor. Together with a 30-inch (0.8-m) wide diaphragm wall, the raft forms a concrete barrier that keeps the site dry.

Loading bay

Commercial vehicles making early morning deliveries to the Sears Tower enter the building via Lower Wacker Drive, which is directly below South Wacker Drive. This docking facility, on lower level 1, contains 15 bays and caters for as many as 40 vehicles which deliver foodstuffs, mail, machinery, and office supplies. Lower level 1 also contains a hair salon, dentist's office, post office, bank vault, and private garage.

Skydeck pavilion

Decorated with flags from around the world, the Skydeck pavilion on Jackson Boulevard welcomes some 1.5 million tourists each year to the world's tallest building. From here, visitors take the elevator down to the ticket area on lower level 2, the Chicago level. After people have been to the "Chicago Experience" slide show and exhibition, high-speed elevators whisk them up to the Skydeck itself. In addition to the tourist attractions, lower level 2 also contains a number of souvenir shops, some plant rooms, and more parking space.

AFTERNOON

In the command center a telephone rings; it is a request for assistance for a visitor in a wheelchair who needs to get down to the garage. This information is passed on to one of the security officers on duty in the lobby, who meets the elevator coming down from the 33rd floor and helps the visitor to a waiting car in the basement.

This request was relayed to the command center by Kathy Huckaby, one of the tenant advocates on the 44th floor. The tenant advocates are a unique feature of the Tower, introduced by the John Buck Company to improve customer care. They are the single point of contact for reporting a light failure, washroom leak, air temperature problem, in fact, any day-to-day problems with the building. Another call comes in, this time from a trader on level 3 saying that it is too hot. Kathy rings the command centre and asks the duty engineer to lower the air temperature in that part of the building. Kathy looks after all tenants up to floor 33, while her counterpart Ann Warren looks after everyone above that. Although it may not appear so, this is an equal split of the floor space and responsibilities.

Unseen by the Skydeck visitors, who are preoccupied with the vast panorama before them, the traffic report station is manned ready for the evening rush hour. Cameras on this and adjoining buildings look down over the grid of streets, pinpointing any traffic congestion. Traffic reports are relayed regularly to the broadcasting networks, whose many aerials and boosters adorn the rooftops of the Tower.

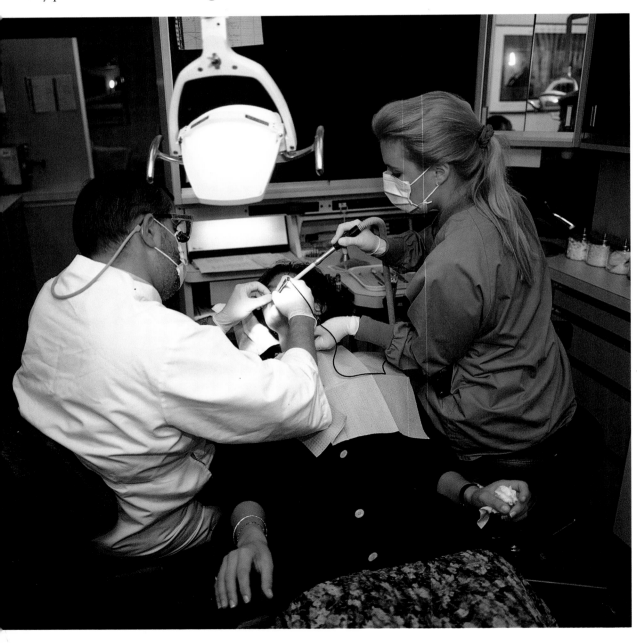

◁ *In his office on lower level 1, dentist Alan Moses tends to a patient, one of the last of the day. It is 3 P.M., and the office will close in an hour—it has been open since 8:30 A.M. without a break for lunch. Alan and his team, of one other dental surgeon and four technicians, see around 30 patients each day, about half of them people who work in the Sears Tower.*

Alan is helped by Karen, his wife and business manager, whose reassuring manner soon puts nervous clients at their ease. If that is not enough, people are offered headphones through which soothing music is played.

Back in his 85th-floor office after lunch in the Metropolitan Club, John Simpson reminisces. "We were taken up the Sears in a wire cage hoist before it was complete. The structure of the building was clearly visible. It was only partially clad and the floors were bare concrete, but we still wanted in, because it was going to become internationally known."

The Tower was never created to seduce the onlooker with decorative motifs. The original lobby entrances were stark, and the outside terraces were bare and bleak. It was designed as the headquarters building for a mail-order company and had to provide efficient accommodation and be economical to run. But when the Sears, Roebuck corporation moved out in 1988, the building suddenly had to appeal to new tenants. The new Sky-deck pavilion made the entrance lobbies, once full of tourists, cafés, and boutiques, far quieter and more welcoming. Now the polished stainless steel on the columns and elevators sparkles, and signposts show the way to tastefully designed restaurants.

Larry Stephens, a partner for the investment brokers Griffin, Kubik, Stephens and Thompson Inc., is open about his firm's reasons for moving into the building recently. Not only does the Tower offer them the right quality of space, its international image is also useful for their out-of-town clients, who like to know where the company is based. As he likes to say, "If you don't know where the Sears Tower is, we don't need you as a client."

△ *The higher, more prestigious, and expensive floors in the Tower are home to some of Chicago's most important law firms and investment brokers. To be high up is to be visible; it also gives tangible expression to your position in the business community. Of course, rent increases as the view improves—it is $32 per square foot above the 50th floor compared to $19 below it.*

Different kinds of business require varying amounts and types of space. The rather functional open-plan trading floor (top) on the 3rd floor is quite unlike the sumptuous walnut-paneled reception area (above) of the law firm on the 85th.

As the sun begins to sink slowly in the sky and the shadows start to lengthen, a line of taxis outside both entrances of the Sears Tower signals the end of the working day. On the dot of 5 P.M., the evening rush begins. But while most people are leaving the building, some are just arriving for work. This is the time when the security officers, engineers, and contractors change over from the day to the night shift. And for traders, such as Cargill Investor Services on the 23rd floor, dealing never stops. As one market closes, another opens on the other side of the world, and this is handled by a different team who work through the night.

This is also the time when the cleaners enter the building, go down to lower level 2, put on their uniforms, and begin to clear away the debris of the day. All of the public areas, from the underground parking facilities to the Skydeck on the 103rd floor, are cleaned each night. Some 75 cleaners—working six-hour shifts between 5 P.M. and 2 A.M.—each vacuum and polish an area of about 32,000 square feet (3,000 m²), equivalent to more than 10 tennis courts. Meanwhile, the hair salon, post office, bank, and newsstand are closing, as are most of the food outlets except for the restaurants. Alan Moses, the dentist, and his wife and business manager, Karen, have long gone; their last appointment finished an hour ago.

In his office on the 44th floor, Philip Domenico, the building manager, looks over the reports from his senior managers on the status of the building. In addition to reading these reports, he also chairs a weekly progress meeting where he can apprise

◁ *The columns of the bundled tube, decorated with sumptuous brushed steel and engraved highlights, dramatically frame the entrance to the Calder lobby (far left). Behind this lobby, which never looks overcrowded even during the rush hour, people are coming out of the elevators on their way home (left).*

The sign "66 to 102" refers to the set of double-decker elevators that travel directly from the ground floor to the skylobbies at floors 66–67. From there, it is possible to take single-decker elevators to any of the floors above.

▷ *It is 5 P.M. and Mrs. Levy's Delicatessen on the concourse has been closed for two hours. Last orders, for a bagel or an all-day brunch, were at 2:30 P.M. Although Eadie's Kitchen and Market is also closed and Caffè Tazza will be shutting in just half an hour, the restaurants are still open and preparing for the early evening rush. The Skydeck, just around the corner, is also open and can be visited until 11 P.M.*

his team of the latest developments. Their discussion ranges from the progress of work on the untenanted floors to the replacement of paving stones damaged during construction of the Skydeck pavilion, new plant-room machinery, emergency fire drills, tenant complaints about air temperature, and spiders.

"Spiders are quite a headache for my staff when they get the wash robots out to clean the building. Hundreds of cobwebs are matted in the gaps in the track, and they have to be removed before cleaning can begin. The spiders are blown onto the building by prevailing winds. In winter they all disappear, but they return again the following spring. They appear to have quite a good lifestyle, judging by their size and the number of insects caught in their webs."

EVENING

Between 7 P.M. and 7 A.M., every visitor to the Sears Tower must pass an I.D. card through a slot at the security desk in the lobby. The information is logged by a computer which can give the security officer on duty in the command center a list of who is still in the building. At 8 P.M. the Mia Torre and Dos Hermanos restaurants close, so that the only place to get food is the Metropolitan Club, where members can be served sandwiches and light meals through to the small hours. The one part of the building still welcoming people is the flag-festooned Skydeck pavilion. After dark, the 103rd-floor observation floor is fairly quiet, although the people who do visit, often young couples, are rewarded with a spectacular view of Chicago laid out below like a jewel-encrusted carpet.

Seven floors above, on the roof, the anemometer reads some 35 mph (55 km/h), and this wind produces a small but perceptible roll. The roof, and the sky around, are lit up 40 times a minute by the rooftop strobe lights which belt out 200,000 candelas of light with each flash to warn aircraft of the presence of a very tall structure. At the other end of the building, on lower level 1, a new group of contractors assemble ready to take their equipment and demolition pallets up in the freight elevator to level 43 to start work. Meanwhile, outside the Wacker Drive entrance, a cleaner guides the machine that washes the day's grime off the granite paving stones.

The front doors of the Tower are officially locked at 10 P.M., along with the loading bay gates on lower level 1. By this time, everything has closed except the souvenir shops and boutiques on lower level 2, which are reached via the Skydeck pavilion and remain open until that shuts at 11 P.M. When the Skydeck closes, all the building's lights are switched off, except in public areas and those floors where tenants are still doing business.

Since electricity is one of the biggest costs, switching the lights off is important. A 13,200-volt substation in lower level 3 provides all the power for the building, which is transformed down to a usable voltage and distributed through its 2,000 miles (3,200 km) of cabling—enough to stretch from New York to Mexico City. At times of peak demand, the Tower guzzles as much power as a town of 35,000 people. "We spend around $8 million per annum on electricity, so we try to be as energy efficient as possible and keep all the machinery in good running order. Recently we changed the main chiller coils from spiral wound to solid fin types, saving 17.5 percent on energy consumption," says Bob Lowe, the mechanical operations manager.

▷ *Out on Lake Michigan, the 35-foot (11-m) single-masted cruiser owned by the John Buck Company skims quietly over the darkening water. At the wheel is Philip Domenico, the building manager, who looks back to see the unmistakable shape of the Sears Tower, stark black against the glowing sunset. Moored in Monroe Harbor, a 10-minute drive from the Tower, the yacht is used for informal socializing with both prospective and existing tenants and staff.*

△ *Security officers maintain a 24-hour vigil over the Tower and those who work there. At night, the officers on duty regularly check that offices and general entry and exit points are secure while keeping in radio contact with the command center. Any person who has not been cleared by security will be challenged, questioned, and escorted from the building.*

LATE NIGHT

◁ *Most of the routine maintenance of the electrical wiring, plumbing, elevator motors and cables, and other machinery is done at night, when the building is quiet and the office community has gone home. The electrical fuses, sprinkler and water pipes, air-conditioning ducts, and lighting systems are all monitored in the command center. Should a fault develop, it can be pinpointed immediately and quickly repaired.*

The massive freight elevator doors slide open to reveal two large gondolas of rubbish being pushed out by the refuse-collection crew. Between 10 P.M. and 4 A.M., just two men work their way around the entire building, collecting the trash bags left in the corridors, piling them into their gondolas, and then emptying them into one of the three 40-cubic-yard (31-m³) compactors in the docking bay on lower level 1. During each nightly clean, the Sears Tower is cleared of around 120 cubic yards (92 m³)—equivalent to a room 13 feet (4 m) square and high—of refuse and building debris from its many offices, stores, and restaurants.

On the 23rd floor, Mike Vaughan is nearing the end of his shift. "I log off at about 2 A.M., having started my shift at 5 P.M. I find night work quite stressful, particularly this evening, as two of my colleagues have cried off sick and I have to cover for them." He works for a trading company, processing data sheets, receiving reports from traders around the world, and logging their transactions on the computer.

"I log off at about 2 A.M., having started my shift at 5 P.M., [and] find the night work quite stressful"

Mike works in the operations room, a well-lit space with one window that looks into the main computer room. Being cut off from a view of the outside world by partition walls and corridors is typical of many offices within the building, especially those on the larger lower floors up to level 50.

One of the security officers on duty in the lobby uses his radio to call the command center with a "10-100" call, which informs his colleague that a short bathroom break is needed. A "10-1" call means officer in trouble, and "10-99" stands for suspicious person—either of these calls would immediately alert every duty officer in the building.

Suddenly, the computer in the command center gives a warning of fire: something has activated the smoke sensors on floors 46 and 47. This automatically sends the whole building system into purge, altering the main fan speed and the output of the chillers and heat pumps for the affected area. Also, to push any smoke out of the building, the air pressure is increased on these floors. Fortunately, Ray, the duty engineer,

◁ *For the trading companies in the building, the working day never ends. As one international stock market closes and one set of people leaves for the day, another shift takes its place at the computers to coincide with the opening of another market.*

For some of the trading companies in the Sears Tower, the working week begins at 2 P.M. on Sunday and finishes at around 11 A.M. the following Saturday. Typically, the trading floors are laid out in orderly rows and are packed with computer screens, keyboards, calculators, telephones, and faxes.

▽ *Every night, the two refuse collectors gather office trash, building debris, and food waste from around the building in their gondolas and dump it into three large compactors. These machines (below), each of which has a 40-cubic-yard (31-m³) capacity, squash the waste and store it ready to be taken away by a garbage truck the following morning.*

knows the reason for the alert. "There are contractors working on those floors, ripping down partitions and ceilings and creating a lot of airborne dust. They are a new team and have forgotten to ring in before starting work to request that the smoke sensors are switched off."

This is the quietest part of the day in the Sears Tower. The whole building is deserted, apart from the refuse-collection men pushing their plastic gondolas of trash around the empty corridors; the security officers checking for open doors, uninvited persons, and suspicious packages; a few teams of contractors and night shift people working in some offices; and the cleaners busy with their domestic chores.

At 1 A.M. Bogulas Walesa, a cleaner of Polish descent, finishes her shift and leaves the building that she has worked in for the last 19 years. Since 7 P.M., when her shift started, she has cleaned all of the third-floor offices by herself. As she walks out onto the street, she turns back to look at the Sears Tower. It is in almost total darkness; only the light from the strobe lights on the roof and the few offices where people are working break the appearance of a slumbering giant.

*"The scenes up here,
out of my windows,
are like a canvas of
ever-changing colors,
breathtaking above
the billowing clouds.
On crystal clear days,
I can see the shoreline
cities across Lake
Michigan to the south,
and toward sunset
the giant shadow of
the Sears reaching out
into the lake."*

JAMES WEISS,
93rd floor

SOARING
AMBITIONS

THE HISTORY OF SKYSCRAPERS

A FIERY BEGINNING

No symbol of the modern world is more compelling than the gravity-defying shafts of steel, glass, and concrete that make up a skyscraper. In the 1890s, a 10-story building was considered a skyscraper, yet only 40 years later, the 102-story Empire State Building was completed. For decades, it was regarded as the ultimate skyscraper, although in time it, too, was overtaken by even taller buildings.

In little more than a century, these structures have risen from 10 to 110 stories and have proliferated to such an extent that they now dominate the skyline of nearly every major city. However, to understand their evolution, a visit to Chicago—the birthplace of the skyscraper—is a must.

Chicago: the cradle of the skyscraper

In the 1820s, Chicago was just a tiny and remote town located on the swampy shore of Lake Michigan. Within 40 years, however, it had become the focal point of commerce in the United States. It is no exaggeration to say that the country's meat and grain prices were determined by the Chicago Board of Trade. The city was also the hub of the national railroad system, which embraced more than 11,000 miles (17,700 km) of track, carried 75 passenger trains a day, and had an annual income of $83 million.

Chicago's development, however, was halted dramatically on the night of 8 October 1871. Around 8 P.M., in Mrs. O'Leary's barn in a Chicago suburb, a cow allegedly

▷ Chicago's worst ever fire was apparently started when a cow knocked over an oil lamp (right). Winds whipped up the flames, which swept through the city destroying everything in their path (far right). In the space of just two days, the inferno had reduced about a third of the city, including the central business district, to smoldering piles of twisted metal and rubble.

kicked over a lamp. Once started, the small blaze was fanned by the persistent breeze and jumped over two rivers, rampaging through the heart of the city. In just 48 hours, the flames had destroyed 18,000 buildings, made 100,000 people homeless, and left 300 people dead.

The so-called fireproof construction of the larger commercial and government buildings had proved to be a tragic joke. In the inferno, exposed cast iron had melted, and the molten iron had set fire to whatever the flames could not reach. The Chicago that rose out of the ashes was more cautious and more conservative. The rebuilding program concentrated on using more durable and robust fireproof materials (and techniques), not the wood and unprotected iron frames of the past.

This large-scale development was the catalyst for proper planning regulations; for the development of new construction methods and materials; for the invention of the elevator; and—with land prices surging so that it was cheaper to build higher rather than to buy a larger plot—eventually led to the birth of the skyscraper.

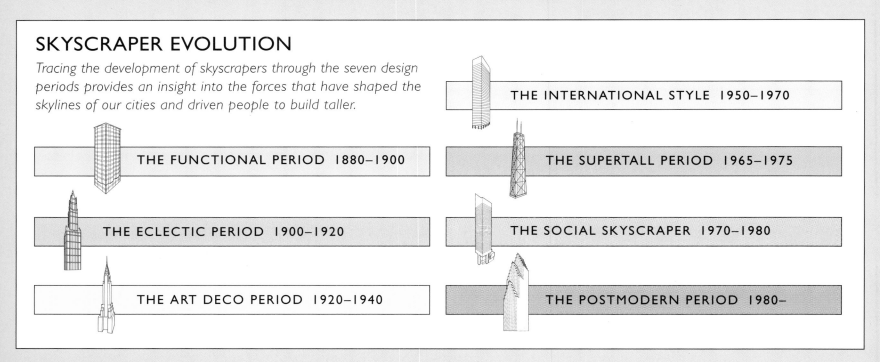

SKYSCRAPER EVOLUTION

Tracing the development of skyscrapers through the seven design periods provides an insight into the forces that have shaped the skylines of our cities and driven people to build taller.

THE FUNCTIONAL PERIOD 1880–1900

THE ECLECTIC PERIOD 1900–1920

THE ART DECO PERIOD 1920–1940

THE INTERNATIONAL STYLE 1950–1970

THE SUPERTALL PERIOD 1965–1975

THE SOCIAL SKYSCRAPER 1970–1980

THE POSTMODERN PERIOD 1980–

▷ MONADNOCK BUILDING 1889

John Wellborn Root's building—the first in Chicago to reach the 17-story mark—is the tallest load-bearing brick structure in the world. Although it has 8-foot (2.4-m) thick walls at the base, the overall impression is not of weight, but of elegance, streamlined proportions, and a pride in being tall.

◁ HOME INSURANCE BUILDING 1885

Generally considered to be the world's first skyscraper, this building was the first to have a lightweight, curtain-wall facade entirely supported by an internal frame made of fireproof iron and steel. Completed in 1885, this 10-story structure set the style for the Chicago School of architecture; it was enlarged in 1891. It was designed by William Le Baron Jenney, one of the most talented structural engineers of the era and a pioneer of early skyscraper construction, and was erected in Chicago as a speculative development. It was demolished in 1931.

THE FUNCTIONAL PERIOD

During the Functional period—the first skyscraper era—there was a revolution in tall-building technology: instead of heavy masonry edifices, there emerged those with a light, steel skeleton and a facade of stone or terracotta. With this lighter structure, larger areas of glass became possible, and the buildings of the period— epitomized by the Reliance Building—were cost-effective and well-engineered, with little decoration. By the end of the period, decoration and glass bay windows characterized high-rise buildings.

Chicago: birthplace of the skyscraper

During the rebuilding of Chicago after the Great Fire, a number of factors came together that gave impetus to the development of skyscrapers. The use of the steel skeleton frame, its separation from the facade, and the widespread use of elevators were all necessary before buildings of more than about five stories became viable.

William Le Baron Jenney

◁ **RELIANCE BUILDING 1895**
Designed by Burnham and Company, the 15-story Reliance Building was a remarkably advanced structure for its time.

It was the first to have a frame made entirely of steel, which meant that the exterior could be sheathed in lightweight, non-load-bearing materials such as glass. This allowed the facade to be built with huge windows framed by terracotta panels and slender piers. Not only was this Chicago building a landmark of the era, it was also constructed amazingly fast—the steel frame for the top 10 stories was erected in just 15 days.

▷ **MASONIC TEMPLE 1892**
This 22-story building, designed by Daniel Burnham and John Wellborn Root, was—at 303 feet (92 m)—the tallest in the world for a short time. It was built in the Romanesque style, evident in the rounded arches, and seems to be less modern and original than other Chicago buildings of the same period. Finished in time for the 1892 World Fair held in Chicago, the Masonic Temple was finally demolished in 1939.

Master architects of the period

Chicago's building bonanza at the turn of the century attracted ambitious architects and innovative designs. Four men dominated the period: William Le Baron Jenney with the Home Insurance Building; Daniel Burnham with the Reliance Building; John Wellborn Root with the Monadnock Building; and, most influential of them all, Louis Henry Sullivan with the Auditorium Building and Carson Pirie Scott Building. These four men, along with the leading firm of Holabird and Roche, were instrumental in establishing the influential architectural movement known as the Chicago School.

Other landmark structures in Chicago included Holabird and Roche's Tacoma Building (1889) and the Manhattan Building completed by Jenney in 1890.

The Equitable Building was New York's only challenge to Chicago's claim to the first skyscraper. Built in 1870, it was the first to have an elevator, but was only six stories tall. The tallest building of the era was Chicago's 22-story Masonic Temple.

HIGH–RISE EVOLUTION

William Le Baron Jenney's use of a steel frame on his Home Insurance Building in 1885 opened a new chapter in building science. It marked the departure from heavy masonry construction. Since this initial development, technology has evolved to such an extent that some of today's designs for the next generation of skyscrapers are reaching 150 stories—15 times the number in Jenney's building.

When deciding on the structure of a skyscraper, the structural engineer, working in conjunction with the architect, has to take a number of criteria into consideration. The structure must be strong enough to resist the forces acting upon it; for instance, it should not sway too much in high winds nor settle excessively under its own weight. In some areas, it must also be resilient enough to absorb earthquake shocks. The entire building should also be as light as possible to keep construction costs low.

The most powerful and variable force affecting skyscrapers is the wind. A tall building acts like a mast anchored in the ground, bending and swaying in the wind. This movement, known as wind drift, should be kept to a minimum so that it does not interfere with the smooth operation of the elevators, crack the external glass or the interior plaster, or make the people inside feel "air sick."

In a well-designed skyscraper, the wind drift should not exceed the height of the building divided by 500. The 1,368-foot (417-m) high World Trade Center in New York, for instance, has a wind drift of just 3 feet (1 m) at the top.

The design of tall buildings took a giant leap upward in the 1960s with the work of the brilliant engineer Fazlur Khan, who pioneered supertall structures. His achievement culminated in the design of two Chicago skyscrapers: the John Hancock Center, a braced framed tube; and the Sears Tower, a bundled tube.

Today, with the help of modern materials and computer analysis, engineers can precisely determine the forces acting on a building and calculate the best structure to use. In many cases, it is possible to make an informed guess about the construction of a modern skyscraper by looking at its shape, the exterior frame, and the arrangement of its windows. Here are some structures in common use today.

◁ *Reliance Building*
Early skyscrapers such as this were designed with a semi-rigid steel frame that depended on the riveted connections.

▷ *225 West Washington*
This stylishly designed modern 28-story building is of the concrete shear core type, but also has a semi-rigid frame.

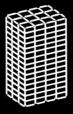

Semi-rigid steel frame
10–15 stories

The floor and frame of the building are connected with rivets or bolts; these form semi-rigid joints which make the frame flexible. This becomes a problem as height increases and the extra wind force leads to twisting and distortion. This type of structure was used on the earliest skyscrapers—those built in Chicago in the late 19th century—and is still in use today for low-rise buildings.

Example: *Reliance Building, Chicago, U.S.A. 1895 (top)*

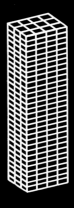

Rigid steel frame
30–40 stories

Similar to the semi-rigid frame, this structure supports a taller building since it has stronger, more rigid connections between the external and internal columns and the floor beams. Developed in the early 1930s, this type of structure is still economical today for smaller skyscrapers.

Example: *Lever House, New York, U.S.A. 1952 (below)*

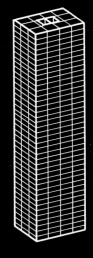

Concrete shear core
40 stories

The central part of the structure is cast as a continuous concrete shaft which acts as a wind brace. The lighter external frame is tied to this central core to stabilize the structure further. Elevators and staircases are installed within the shaft.

Example: *225 West Washington, Chicago, U.S.A. 1986 (top)*

◁ *Lever House*
The strength of this building is derived from the rigid plate connections that join the external and interior

◁ **METROPOLITAN LIFE TOWER 1909**
*When the plans for the 700-foot (213-m) tall
Metropolitan Life Tower were published, they
caused a storm. Although architect Pierre
LeBrun, from the firm of Napoleon LeBrun
and Sons, denied the charge, his tower did
closely resemble the Campanile, or bell tower,
in St. Mark's Square, Venice (above). Such
blatant copying of a famous historical building
was without precedent.*

*Whatever the origin of the design, the
building, with its three-story-high clock
face, was a handsome and easily identifiable
addition to the New York skyline. And it was
exactly what the directors of the Metropolitan
Life Company had wanted, since it represented
stability in a volatile market and echoed the
qualities of past cultures.*

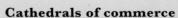

©1913 by Equitable C

Cathedrals of commerce

The second decade of the 20th century, the peak of the
eclectic age, produced some of the most memorable
and remarkable skyscrapers. By then, putting up tall
buildings using steel sections and mechanically driven
hoists and cranes was second nature to the building
industry in the United States.

Building owners and their architects began to explore
new architectural styles which combined height and
decoration in a way that would reflect the owner's
corporate status or aspirations. In New York, the spiritual
home of the eclectic skyscraper, money was no object, and
buildings expressed the power of wealth and position.

△ **TIMES BUILDING 1904**
*Under construction in a corner of Times Square is the Times
Building by Cyrus L.W. Eidlitz. The heavy steel frame of the box
columns and girder beams has been completed to the 17th floor
and the stone cladding is in place on the lower half. Although, at
375 feet (114 m), it was taller than the Flatiron Building and was
built on a site with a similar shape, this structure never achieved
the same popularity. It is also the tallest building ever to have
been demolished in New York.*

Setting the scene

In the late 19th century, wheeler-dealers like John Jacob Astor
and Cornelius Vanderbilt made their fortunes in real estate,
shipping, and railroads. They appreciated big ideas and saw
skyscrapers as flagships for their ambitions. They also wanted
New York to be the center for new business in the United States.
The race was on to outstrip Chicago and make New York the
first city of tall buildings.

The drop in steel prices, lack of planning regulations, and the
legendary ability of the local Mohawk Indian steeplejacks to keep
their balance when working at great heights all fueled the race to
build taller. Such was the prestige of high-rise buildings that some
were far taller than was economically sensible. Often, they were
also totally insensitive to the environment in which they stood and
to the effect of their towering presence on the surrounding area.

The first New York flagships

In 1895, the 306-foot (93-m) American Surety Building snatched
the title of the world's tallest building from Chicago's Masonic
Temple by a whisker and took it to New York, where it remained,
held by many different buildings, for more than 70 years.

Skyscraper building, however, really took off in New York after
1900. In 1903, the ever-popular Flatiron Building was completed,
and five years later, the slender tower of the Singer Building
caused a stir by breaking the 600-foot (183-m) mark, overtaking
its nearest rival, the Times Building, by some 237 feet (73 m).

◁ FLATIRON BUILDING 1903

This remarkable creation, located on Madison Square, is one of the most famous, instantly recognizable, and popular buildings in New York. Designed by Daniel Burnham, it is a sheer triangular tower that is only 6 feet (1.8 m) wide at its apex. The steel frame, which by then dominated skyscraper construction, allowed Burnham greater flexibility in his choice of external decoration. Thus the tower is clad in an ornate blanket of limestone blocks that are decorated in the French Renaissance style, creating a clarity of structural expression that was rare at that time.

A symbol of the city, Flatiron drew the attention of artists and photographers. For many young men, however, part of its attraction was the fact that downdrafts created by the building caused ladies' petticoats to lift as they walked by.

▷ SINGER BUILDING 1908

When completed, Ernest Flagg's steel-framed 612-foot (187-m) tall Singer Building was the tallest in the world, topping all existing skyscrapers by nearly 250 feet (76 m). This great height assured grander views, cleaner air, and escape from the polluted streets below in a city where row upon row of 15- and 20-story buildings lined the streets and blocked out the light.

The Singer Building's soaring slender tower was covered in ornate brick and terracotta in the French beaux-arts fashion. It was topped with a mansard roof that would not have been out of place in Florence. For a building that represented such a breakthrough in building height, it was odd to see such a mixed bag of architectural styles.

THE ECLECTIC PERIOD

Building design and decoration became increasingly flamboyant in the first decades of the new century. The restrained elegance and order of the Chicago skyscraper were superseded by the exuberance of Gothic and Renaissance motifs imported from Europe and grafted onto a growing colony of monuments to capitalism. Based in New York, this exciting and dynamic style was epitomized by two buildings: Daniel Burnham's Flatiron Building (1903) and Cass Gilbert's Woolworth Building (1913).

LOUIS HENRY SULLIVAN

The architectural father of the skyscraper was Louis Henry Sullivan (1856–1924). He exploited the new technology of the steel-frame building, expressing it as an art form. He also wrote with eloquence about the architecture of the tall building and what he personally was striving to achieve.

From an early age, Sullivan showed a talent for drawing and a love of the outdoors; indeed, his study of nature had a profound influence on his architectural style. He studied at the Massachusetts Institute of Technology, then worked for various architectural practices, including that of William Le Baron Jenney, until, in 1881, he formed a partnership with Dankmar Adler, an engineer and architect. With Adler solving the engineering problems, they worked on more than 200 projects and designed some of the most important buildings constructed in Chicago between 1880 and 1895. Although the partnership broke up during the economic depression of 1895, Sullivan continued to practice alone for another 30 years.

Sullivan hated "phoney" buildings and argued against the use of borrowed styles. He was an idealist with a clear idea about the role of architecture in society: to him every building was unique, with a spirit that must be reflected in its design. He felt that until a civilization had produced good architecture, it could not produce a good life for its citizens, and maintained that an architect should try to enhance human satisfaction and purpose within a building. All Sullivan's architecture reflected this lifelong search for social order and perfection of form, and he strove both to embody this idea of democratic architecture, or "Functionalism," in his buildings and to explain it in his writings.

Many of Sullivan's designs are still revered as some of the most skillful and brilliant of any high-rise era. His masterpieces, which include the Wainwright and the Carson Pirie Scott buildings, still bear testimony to his ideals.

△ **AUDITORIUM BUILDING 1889**
Besides being the most massive and the most expensive building of the period, Louis Sullivan's Auditorium Building in Chicago was remarkable for its exquisite interior. The theater is based on a series of arches, with decorative murals and motifs finished in exquisite gold leaf laid over rich background colors.

◁ **WAINWRIGHT BUILDING 1891**
Although this building in St. Louis was not tall—it was only 10 stories—Sullivan's design gave it a remarkable sense of height. He emphasized the vertical lines, the piers, by recessing the horizontal element, the windows. This also helped overcome the squareness of the shape by lifting the eye over the perfectly proportioned brick and terracotta facade. The ornate cornice and the decorative panels under the windows balance with the smooth verticals and help to complete this study in total design.

◁ **GUARANTY BUILDING 1895**
Many architectural historians consider the Guaranty Building (now the Prudential Building) in Buffalo to be Sullivan's greatest achievement in partnership with Adler. It is a soaring display of skillfully proportioned piers and recessed windows that transform a rather squat shape into an elegant tower. This was achieved in much the same way as it was in the Wainwright Building, but the cornice is less overbearing and appears to grow out of the swirling decoration. The innovative design of the front windows, which are inclined at the top, seems to lift the entire building up into the air.

△ **CARSON PIRIE SCOTT BUILDING 1904**
Sullivan's last major work, his swan song as a social architect and the final achievement of the Functional era, was the Carson Pirie Scott department store. His thoroughness, and the clarity with which he exploited the sleek lines, slender proportions, and overall shape, put Sullivan in a league of his own.

The emphasis was on the long horizontal elevations; only the rounded tower above the entrance stressed the vertical element. The facade was covered in white-glazed tiles and featured large windows to let in as much light as possible. Sullivan's ornamentation of the entrance and lower levels in cast iron was magnificent. The building remains a masterpiece; its power, grace, and dignity transcend the passage of time and the limited technology of the period.

Steel-framed tube
90–100 stories

The perimeter columns and beams form a
closely spaced grill of steel that runs the full
height of the building. This lattice is connected
to the internal frame of more columns and
floor beams to create a rigid box or tube structure which is very strong and can absorb all the
wind and gravity forces.

Example: **World Trade Center,
New York, U.S.A. 1972** *(left)*

Exterior-braced framed tube
100 stories

An advance on the steel-framed tube, this
design adds cross-bracing to the perimeter
framed tube to increase the rigidity of the
structure. The downward force of gravity and
sideward force of the wind are shared between
the outer frame and inner columns.

Example: **John Hancock Center,
Chicago, U.S.A. 1969** *(left below)*

Bundled tube
120 stories

A cluster of framed tubes, interconnected at
their common sides, forms a lightweight yet
immensely strong structure that can reach well
over 100 stories.

Example: **Sears Tower, Chicago, U.S.A.
1974** *(right top)*

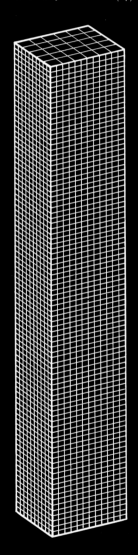

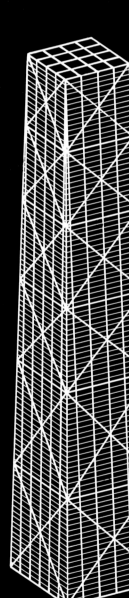

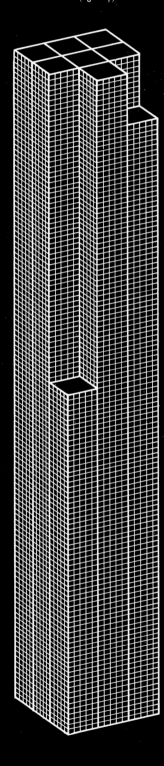

◁ **John Hancock Center**
*The cross-bracing on the exterior of this skyscraper
gives a dramatic feeling of height and strength. It was an
innovative way of bolstering the exterior framed tube.*

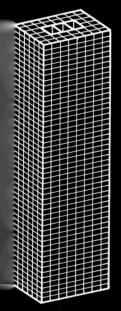

...med concrete shear core
50 stories

...ension of the concrete shear ...his type of structure works by ... the core, the external frame, ...he floors act together to ...ze the wind resistance. This ...buildings to rise a further 10 ...without a dramatic increase in ...ts of construction.

...ple: **Natwest Bank Tower, London, U.K. 1980**

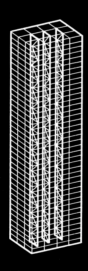

Steel-framed shear truss
40 stories

The external frame alone is not rigid enough to withstand the force of the wind without swaying excessively. To increase the rigidity, vertical shear trusses are positioned on opposite sides of the building exterior and in the core. These trusses are light yet strong steel stiffening frames that resemble braced ladders. This type of design was the basis for many of the most famous eclectic skyscrapers including the Woolworth, Chrysler, and Empire State buildings, but uses as much as 30 percent more steel than modern designs.

Example: **Chicago Civic Center, Chicago, U.S.A. 1965** *(top)*

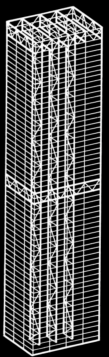

Steel belt truss with framed shear truss
60 stories

With this design, sturdy horizontal trusses are incorporated at strategic levels up the building to enhance the effectiveness of the framed shear truss. Each horizontal truss spans an entire floor, enclosing the perimeter steel, and acts rather like a belt that ties in the upper and lower stories.

Example: **First Wisconsin Center, Milwaukee, U.S.A. 1974** *(top)*

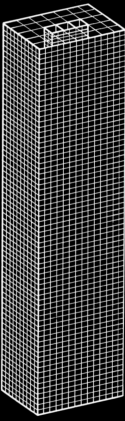

Concrete tube-in-tube
70 stories

A development of the steel-framed tube, this is an entirely concrete structure that consists of two wind-resisting boxes—one on the outside and one in the center of the building. Each tube is made up of a grid of columns and interconnecting beams which combine to transfer all the forces on the building down into the foundations.

Example: **Olympia Center, Chicago, U.S.A. 1986**

Steel truss tube with mega columns
130 stories

Stronger steel, precisely engineered connections, and tubular corner sections filled with concrete form the external frame of this structure. It is rigid and strong, yet quite a lightweight megastructure.

Example: **Landmark Tower, Yokohama, Japan 1993** (right bottom)

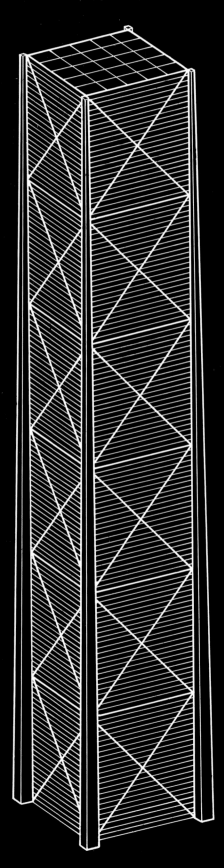

Superframe
150 stories

This innovative structure combines a number of framed tubes connected by horizontal framed trusses, almost like a series of Eiffel Towers strapped together. Although an example has yet to be built, these mega-structures will make it possible to build skyscrapers of at least 150 stories.

△ *Sears Tower*
Nine steel-framed tubes were bundled together to produce this light but strong supertall building. When completed in 1974, it took the title as the world's tallest building.

△ *Landmark Tower*
The prominent steel columns on the corners of this building reinforce the truss tube structure and enable it to withstand wind and seismic forces.

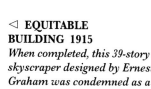

◁ **EQUITABLE BUILDING 1915**

When completed, this 39-story skyscraper designed by Ernest Graham was condemned as a giant box in which to crate people; a menace to public health and safety; and an offense which had to be stopped. With 1.2 million square feet (111,500 m²) of floor space—creating a glut of office space—it was by far the largest building in the world and cast a shadow that was more than four blocks long.

The Equitable Building has the dubious distinction of being at least in part responsible for the introduction, in the year following its completion, of planning laws to regulate skyscraper design. From 1916, New York skyscrapers were limited to a total floor area not more than 12 times the size of the plot—this building was almost three times that size.

▷ **MUNICIPAL BUILDING 1913**

McKim, Mead and White's scheme was the winning entry in a competition to design a building to house New York's burgeoning bureaucracy. This U-shaped building, liberally endowed with Classical motifs, was not especially innovative, although the presence of a subway entrance inside it was a model for generations of buildings to come.

Motifs from a multitude of styles, including Gothic cathedrals, Palladian villas, Greek temples, Renaissance palaces, and French chateaux, were molded onto the skyscrapers of this period with great ingenuity and skill. Some of the results, however, were ugly, out-of-scale edifices that blighted their surroundings. The most famous of these, the Equitable Building, caused such outrage that in 1916 regulations were introduced to restrict the worst excesses. From that time, as height increased, building profiles had to be set back to limit the shadows they cast.

Notable buildings of the era

Historical reference reached a new extreme in 1909 with the 700-foot (213-m) tall Metropolitan Life Tower. It appeared to be based on the Campanile in St. Mark's Square, Venice. Despite some controversy, this building inspired several others in the same shape: Trowbridge and Livingstone's 1912 creation, the Bankers Trust Company Building, also in New York, had a pyramidal top to the tower and Ionic colonnades; and in Boston, the Customs House Tower (1915), designed by Peabody and Stearns, is rather overloaded with Classical references.

By contrast, New York's Municipal Building of 1913 was innovative not because of its height or style, but because it interacted well with the immediate environment. But the greatest skyscraper of the eclectic period was Cass Gilbert's glorious Woolworth Building, completed in 1913. At 792 feet (241 m), it was also the tallest building in the world at the time.

WOOLWORTH BUILDING

The outstanding masterpiece of the eclectic period was the Woolworth Building, designed by Cass Gilbert and completed in 1913. Gilbert was familiar with medieval Gothic architecture, since he had studied in Europe, and he had no hesitation in using Gothic models for the building. "To me a skyscraper, by its height, which makes its upper parts appear lost in the clouds, is a monument whose masses must become more and more inspired the higher it rises. The Gothic style gave us the possibility of expressing the greatest degree of aspiration...the ultimate note of the mass gradually gaining in spirituality the higher it mounts."

Here was a building of superb visual richness, plagiarized from 12th-century Christian Europe, which dealt with the special problems of scale and height with consummate skill. The lines of white terracotta soared vertically from the base to the tower, fusing the upper and lower elements, and—unusually—the presence of Gothic motifs, terracotta gargoyles and buttresses was subsumed in the unity of the building's proportions and its dramatic verticality.

The Gothic heritage was also emphasized in the interior, with the high vaulted ceilings of the corridors and the sumptuous lobby. Its walls were lined with veined marble from Skyros, and the elevator doors and canopies were embossed with lacelike patterns of wrought iron to simulate stone tracery.

The combination of delicate ornament on

◁ *Cass Gilbert (1859–1934), seen here in 1927, studied both at the Massachusetts Institute of Technology and in Europe.*

In 1880 he started work as a draftsman with the New York architects McKim, Mead and White, then three years later set up a partnership in St. Paul, Minnesota. His design for the state capitol there brought him acclaim, and he moved back to New York in 1899.

In addition to the Woolworth, he produced such notable buildings as the New York Life Insurance Building and Washington's Supreme Court Building; he was also consulting architect for the George Washington Bridge.

the rooftop cornices, the grace of the tower, and the strength of the overall design captured popular imagination. Indeed, the Reverend Samuel Parkes Cadman, when he first set eyes on the building, called it the "Cathedral of Commerce" and was moved to write, "It inspires feelings even too deep for tears." Delighted, the Woolworth Company adopted the epithet for the title of a brochure, published in 1917, which described the building, complete with many astonishing facts.

Standing 792 feet (241 m) high, the building cost $13.5 million to construct and was paid for in cash. It housed 14,000 workers, contained 2,800 telephones, and had 29 of the fastest elevators in the world. The coal bunker in the basement could store 2,000 tons of coal for its boilers, which generated 2,500 horsepower for the heating system. The Woolworth Building was acknowledged, by visitors and critics alike, as a graceful mixture of delicacy and strength—the Queen of all Manhattan.

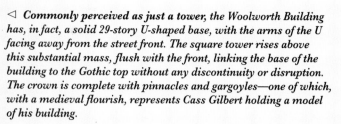

◁ **Commonly perceived as just a tower, the Woolworth Building has, in fact, a solid 29-story U-shaped base, with the arms of the U facing away from the street front. The square tower rises above this substantial mass, flush with the front, linking the base of the building to the Gothic top without any discontinuity or disruption. The crown is complete with pinnacles and gargoyles—one of which, with a medieval flourish, represents Cass Gilbert holding a model of his building.**

△ **In this photograph of a side lobby, taken in 1947, the wrought-iron pattern and detailing on the ceiling show some of the glory of the interior of the building.**

With its splendid vaulted arches, walls of sumptuous marble, masses of intricate detailing, and soft ceiling decoration, the main entrance lobby resembles a Gothic cathedral. The new American Gothic, bigger and better than the European original, had arrived with a vengeance.

▷ WRIGLEY BUILDING 1921

Financed by William Wrigley's five-cent chewing gum empire, this building (in the center of the photograph) was designed by Graham, Anderson, Probst and White. It consists of a 17-story base, topped by a slender 11-story clock tower that is based on the Moorish and Renaissance Giralda Tower in Seville, Spain. It was constructed with a semi-rigid steel frame, resting on hand-dug caisson foundations, and was inspired by McKim, Mead and White's Municipal Building of 1913.

Six different shades of enamel, varying from gray to cream, were baked onto the terracotta facade, becoming lighter toward the top. When it was illuminated, this coloring made the whole building resemble a gleaming white castle.

▷ TRIBUNE TOWER 1925

Raymond Hood and John Mead Howells's Gothic Revival design for the Tribune Tower (far right of photograph) beat more than 250 other entries from around the world to win the Chicago Tribune's 1922 competition. The owners of the newspaper wanted a building that would symbolize the power and authority of the Tribune, advance the art of architecture, and provide them with an efficient headquarters. In their eyes, it had to be the most beautiful office building in the world.

The result was a handsome 34-story, 462-foot (141-m) tall building, with a crown of flying buttresses and open tracery that was inspired by the famed Butter Tower of Rouen Cathedral, France. It required complex engineering, including caisson foundations that were dug into the bedrock to support the steel-column and girder-frame structure.

THE ART DECO PERIOD

An extension of the eclectic style, Art Deco involved greater imagery, flamboyance, and color. It originated in Europe in the 1920s and had developed into a major style by the 1930s. The name was derived from the Exposition Internationale des Arts Décoratifs et Industriels Modernes held in Paris in 1925. Art Deco was a wonderful mixture of diverse styles, including past European fashion; Mayan, Aztec, and Chinese architecture; and the modern influences of Cubism, Futurism, and Expressionism. In architecture, these influences were all brought together to heighten the drama and sensual expression of the tall building, creating such great examples as the fabulous Chrysler Building and the Empire State Building—the most famous skyscraper of all time.

The roaring twenties

This decade was the era of Prohibition, organized crime, and Al Capone, as well as the dawn of the jazz age. It was a period of intense rivalry between New York, the country's financial capital, and Chicago, the center of its meat and grain markets; and each tried to claim the title of "supreme city of the skyscraper." More than ever, tall buildings were a status symbol.

While Art Deco was the style of the era, there was a growing mood among architects—especially after the competition to design the Tribune Tower in Chicago—that rejected the derivative designs of eclecticism and yearned for pure architecture. It was, however, another 20 years before the simpler Modern, or International, Style began to dominate skyscraper design.

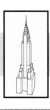

△ NEW YORK TELEPHONE BUILDING 1926
Also known as the Barclay–Vesey Building because of its location at the intersection of these streets, this building is one of the most important examples of Art Deco architecture. The setbacks and monochrome exterior were ahead of their time and hint at the non-derivative modernist architecture first advocated by the Finnish architect Eliel Saarinen in his second-place entry for the Chicago Tribune competition. By contrast, the inside was finished in an orgy of dazzling adornment and color typical of Art Deco.

▷ HELMSLEY BUILDING 1929
Originally called the New York Central Building, this building straddles Park Avenue, with traffic passing through two huge arches in its base. Now offset by the giant Met Life Building, formerly the Pan Am Building, its pyramidal crown and cupola act as the focal point for the streets below.

Superstructures of the era
In addition to Chicago's Tribune Tower, landmark buildings of the period included the New York Telephone Building and Raymond Hood's American Radiator, now American Standard, Building, also in New York. Completed in 1924, the latter had a similar shape to the Tribune Tower, but it tapered in steps toward the top. This sleek black building with gold decoration seemed more elegant and taller than its mere 21 stories.

In terms of height, Woolworth still reigned supreme; only the 680-foot (207-m) tall Chanin Building came close to beating it. By this time, every city skyline in the United States was dominated by skyscrapers in a mixture of styles.

◁ **CHRYSLER BUILDING 1930**
Beloved symbol of New York for more than 60 years, the Chrysler Building has weathered the cycles of taste more successfully than any other. William Van Alen's romantic and fantastic design is based on the automobile motif of the client; the spire of stainless-steel arches punctuated by triangular windows is inspired.

Although sneered at by some architects, this jewel of the Art Deco period embodied the energy, flamboyance, and drive of the age. The tower of white glazed brick, with gray trim and gargoyles posted on the corners (shown above nearing completion), fused perfectly with the well-proportioned base. Inside, the lobby was finished in African red marble, and the elevator doors were richly inlaid with cherry wood.

Advances in technology

Over the decades, tall-building technology moved on so far that 100-story skyscrapers became possible. Shear-core, shear-truss, and framed-tube structures were all developed as engineers and architects gained a better understanding of the forces acting on a building. And higher-grade steel, thicker-plate girders, better-riveted connections, and machine-excavated pile and caisson foundations all allowed greater forces to be carried.

New elevator designs meant that fewer shafts were needed in a building, leaving more usable floor space and so increasing the economic viability of tall buildings. Other improvements, such as forced ventilation, fluorescent lighting, and pressurized hot-water systems, all raised the level of comfort within tall buildings.

▷ *At the Beaux-Arts Ball held in 1931, the theme was "Fête Moderne." For one scene, called "Skyline of New York," leading architects dressed up as their own creations. William Van Alen's costume, admired here by his wife, captured the essence of his Chrysler Building.*

▽ **ROCKEFELLER CENTER 1932–40**
Everything that 1920s and '30s architecture had been striving to achieve came together with the vast project for Rockefeller Center, which was designed by a consortium of leading architects. Set in central New York, this complex of tower blocks, plazas, theaters, and stores had a coherent feeling of a city within a city.

The centerpiece of the massive development was the 70-storey RCA Building (left). Largely the work of Raymond Hood, it was a sheer wall of Indiana limestone with cascading setbacks. Its sleek, slablike vertical planes, which emphasized the power of the composition, were a new departure for skyscraper design. Despite its size, the RCA Building still managed to harmonize with the surrounding family of tall buildings—it was not an isolated tower like so many of New York's skyscrapers.

The last megaliths

On 29 October 1929, the Wall Street Crash heralded an economic depression that lasted a decade and was followed by World War II. Despite this, some of the buildings that had been commissioned in the late 1920s were still completed. In 1930, the Manhattan Company Bank Building, designed by Craig Severance, became the world's tallest building at 927 feet (283 m). Within a month, however, the 1,046-foot (319-m) tall Chrysler Building had taken the title. Chrysler was to have been just 925 feet (282 m) tall, but William Van Alen was determined to have the record and had a new, taller spire assembled in secret.

Even before the Chrysler Building was completed, construction was underway for a tower to dwarf them all. The Empire State Building, completed in 1931, stood at 1,250 feet (381 m) and was the world's tallest building for four decades. For height, it could not be beaten; but for sheer size and vision, Rockefeller Center was the biggest development ever undertaken.

The battle of ideology

Architects were divided about the style of buildings throughout this period. Those who supported the new pure form, which was currently gaining acceptance in Europe, were increasingly in charge, yet most of their clients clung to the romance of eclecticism. The last monuments of the era, the Chrysler and Empire State buildings, left an indelible mark on the urban landscape—one which still endures today.

EMPIRE STATE BUILDING

New York in 1931 was a place very different from the city of the 1920s. The Wall Street Crash had wiped out many of the money barons and shaken this center of opportunity and enterprise. The Empire State Building, which had been commissioned as a speculative investment during New York's heady days, rose like a rocket from the corner of 33rd Street. This 102-story structure, which reached 1,250 feet (381 m), was the world's tallest and most celebrated skyscraper. It is said that on a clear day you can see for 80 miles (130 km) from the 102nd floor. To many of New York's residents and visitors today, this is still the greatest skyscraper ever built and is the building that everyone comes to see.

Construction commenced on 17 March 1930, and the structure grew at a rate of four and a half stories each week. In just 410 days, the building was completed—a record for the fastest construction ever. It is also the only skyscraper in the world to be built for less than its original budget (which was $50 million).

△ *Flirting with danger was routine for the "sky boys" constructing the Empire State Building. Here, in one of a series of romanticized photographs by Lewis Hine, the workers, with negligible safety protection, are riveting a steel connection plate to a perimeter column.*

A steel frame weighing 60,000 tons supported the building, which was finished with 10 million bricks and 730 tons of aluminum and stainless steel.

John Jacob Raskob, founder of General Motors, headed the five-man consortium that commissioned Shreve, Lamb and Harmon to design the office building. Although the styling was not as dazzling as that of the Chrysler, it was just as well proportioned. The progressive setbacks of the base, middle, and tower sections were necessary to comply with zoning laws to reduce the shadow line on neighboring buildings. But these, together with the hint of Art Deco in the aluminum and nickel trim over the windows as well as the scalloped masthead, all increase the dramatic impact of the building.

Today, the Empire State Building houses about 15,000 people who work for more than 850 companies with bases in six continents. Seventy-three elevators travel through 7 miles (11 km) of elevator shafts to whisk people out of the lobby and up into the building, although they could walk up the 1,860 steps to the top. It also contains 70 miles (113 km) of water pipes and 2½ million feet (762,000 m) of electrical cable.

△ *The three-story lobby is lined with 10,000 square feet (930 m²) of Rose Famosa and Estrallante marble. It is dominated by this towering brass relief of the building which is inscribed on the base "The eighth wonder of the world."*

◁ *A golden glow suffuses the tower when sunlight catches it, but at night it is really spectacular. Thousands of lights around the top of the building act as a fluorescent calendar, changing color to mark national holidays and major events throughout the year. For instance, the mast is lit up in red, white, and blue for the Fourth of July; green for St. Patrick's Day; and (far left) red and green for Christmas.*

KING KONG

In 1933, the Empire State was the scene of a cinematic battle to the death. The fight featured King Kong astride the mast of the building, grabbing wildly at the biplanes that were shooting at him. The dramatic New York skyline provided the backdrop.

59

◁ **LEVER HOUSE 1952**
Although not a tall building, Lever House was the first in a line of innovative glass towers that changed the face of skyscraper architecture for decades to come. The design, by Gordon Bunshaft of Skidmore, Owings & Merrill, consisted of two glass and steel blocks: one lying horizontally on columns to make an open plaza; the other placed vertically on top of it.

▷ **SEAGRAM BUILDING 1958**
Mies van der Rohe's first major skyscraper, the Seagram Building, is set back from New York's Park Avenue above a two-story glass-enclosed lobby. The tower of bronzed glass, which rises 38 stories above the street, has been acclaimed as the finest glass tower ever built.

The building is seen as the fulfillment of Mies's philosophy and an icon of the period. The structural purity of the steel frame is boldly expressed behind the glass facade.

The Seagram Building and Lever House were so admired at the time that the zoning laws of New York and Chicago were changed to encourage similar buildings. But the policy has since proved unpopular, as glass boxes have proliferated unchecked.

THE INTERNATIONAL STYLE

Developed in Europe in the early decades of the century, the International Style was spread to the United States by refugees, such as Mies van der Rohe, fleeing World War II. During the 1950s, the style, whose name is derived from the catalog for an architectural exhibition held at New York's Museum of Modern Art, became the dominant architectural ideology. The new commercial citadels had to be economical and functional; they were usually box-shaped, made of glass, steel, and concrete, and stripped of all decoration. The purity of the form was realized in only a handful of buildings, the best of which was the Seagram Building.

A new beginning

The end of World War II promised a new era of peace and prosperity. Expectations were high, and so were living standards and construction costs. Traditional crafts skills, however, had all but gone, and labor costs and land prices had risen so much that eclectic buildings were commercial suicide. The glass box was the way forward and, from the 1950s, it began to dominate every major city in the world. Modern office space, such as the Seagram Building and Lever House, was what clients wanted, or so the architects thought. Some architects, however, made this style seem banal and bland, especially when developers insisted on economy rather than quality.

△ **CENTRO PIRELLI 1958**
Designed by Giovanni Ponti—an Italian architect who also painted and designed for the theater—and executed by the great Italian engineer Pier Luigi Nervi, this beautiful, hexagonal glass tower is the headquarters of the Pirelli Tire Company in Milan, Italy. Its slenderness is accentuated by the tapering side walls, and its height—420 feet (128 m)—made it the second tallest building in Europe at the time.

The high priest of modern architecture
Mies van der Rohe (1886–1969) believed in design innovation and purity of form, seen through a glass facade. His vision, inspired by Walter Gropius and others at the Bauhaus school, of which Mies became a director in 1930, led to a new design ideology. Architectural expression was reduced to the essence of structural form, relying on shape and scale to achieve elegance and beauty.

His legacy is still reflected in the output of many established architects and practices. These include Skidmore, Owings & Merrill, a firm he helped to set up; I.M. Pei; Roche and Dinkeloo; Philip Johnson, his devoted disciple and assistant on the Seagram Building; and others who came in contact with his genius when he was professor at the Illinois Institute of Technology in Chicago.

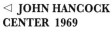

◁ **JOHN HANCOCK CENTER 1969**
Nicknamed "Big John," this 100-story tower, designed by Fazlur Khan (above), dominates the skyline of downtown Chicago. The strength needed to make this 1,127-foot (344-m) giant stable was achieved extremely economically by placing most of the steel on the outside of the structure, where it acts as a wind brace. Some $15 million was saved just on the conventional steelwork by using these huge cross braces.

The John Hancock Center is the world's tallest mixed-use skyscraper, combining a hotel with offices, stores, and private apartments. It also contains a fitness center and a large swimming pool on the 40th floor.

THE SUPERTALL PERIOD

During the 1960s, the image of the skyscraper re-emerged as one of economic prowess and might. This return to the individualism of the 1920s can be attributed as much to innovation in the technology of tall buildings as to the growing dissatisfaction with the uniform glass-box look. The development of high-grade steel, fusion-welded sections, and new types of connections offered enormous potential for saving weight and with it construction time and money, especially when combined with some of the new designs for megastructures. Leading light and pioneer of the bundled tube was Fazlur Khan, who worked for Skidmore, Owings & Merrill in Chicago. He designed the John Hancock Center and the Sears Tower, two of the most innovative tall structures ever seen.

◁ **SEARS TOWER 1974**
The structure of this record-breaking 1,454-foot (443-m) tall building is a bundled tube, in which the perimeter columns brace the building against the wind—the natural enemy of all skyscrapers. Since the nine tubes that make up the building terminate at various heights, the Sears Tower has a stepped appearance that sits somewhere between the glass box and the tapering tops of eclectic structures. The black anodized coating on the steel and the tinted glass panels soften the face of this lofty giant to create the illusion of transparency.

△ **WORLD TRADE CENTER 1972**
Despite the building's colossal dullness, Minoru Yamasaki's twin towers made use of a number of structural innovations. The outside skin was designed as a steelwork mesh that supported a large proportion of the building's weight. In some ways, this advanced structure actually harked back to the shear truss of the Empire State and Rockefeller Center, and even to the load-bearing walls of the earliest Chicago skyscrapers. Dominating the Manhattan skyline, the two towers do, at least, work quite well together as a kind of stark sculpture.

Searching for a new philosophy

The debasement of the International Style created mediocrity in architecture and monotony of style. The 1960s and '70s became a period of discussion about styles. On one side were the Modernists, who remained loyal to Mies van der Rohe's philosophy of minimalist architecture. In Chicago, C.F. Murphy finished the Richard Daley Center in 1965 and, around the same time, Mies himself finished the Federal Center. On the other side were the early Postmodernists and Romantic Modernists, who wanted to revive the symbolism and ornamentation associated with more eclectic architecture.

While architects were discussing the future of architecture, the skyscraper was going through a revival. Building developers and owners once again became interested in tall buildings. After a break of nearly 40 years, there was a new drive for height.

High and mighty

Advances in engineering made it economically viable to challenge the Empire State as the world's tallest building. In 1969, the John Hancock Center in Chicago came within 130 feet (40 m) of the title. But it was only in 1972 that the record was broken by New York's World Trade Center at 1,368 feet (417 m). Two years later, however, the Sears Tower took this much coveted title back to Chicago—it had been in New York since 1895. Elsewhere in the world, Maine Montparnasse reached 751 feet (229 m) in Paris, and the 935-foot (285-m) First Bank Tower was built in Toronto.

DEFYING NATURE

Skyscrapers must be built to endure the ravages of climate and environment: hurricane-force winds, lightning, rain, and hailstones; freezing and frying temperatures; earthquakes and air-borne pollution. Because of this, they are, reassuringly, among the safest and strongest structures built today.

△ **TRANSAMERICA PYRAMID 1972**
William Pereira's skyscraper in San Francisco is celebrated for its ability to resist earthquakes, which it owes to its flexible steel frame that allows the building to absorb vibrations. The cladding—composed of glass windows set within reinforced concrete panels—means that the building is also rigid enough to withstand the force of the wind.

When San Francisco is hit by an earthquake, for instance, one of the buildings least likely to be damaged is the 853-foot (260-m) high Transamerica Pyramid. The foundations of this building rest on bedrock, so they are not seriously disturbed when the soft subsoil above is shaken by seismic waves. And above ground, the structure is not only isolated from the foundations by heavy-duty shock absorbers that lessen the tremors that reach them, but it is also designed to absorb any vibrations over the miles of steelwork in its frame.

As buildings have become taller, the wind has become more of a problem. When it hits a building, all of its force is directed onto one side. With tall buildings, the larger wall area means that a greater force must be absorbed and transferred to the foundations. It is little wonder, then, that more than 30 percent of the steel structure in modern skyscrapers is for wind-bracing. The use of wind-tunnel tests and computer analysis has allowed engineers to design rigid structures that can resist the strongest winds, yet do not use much extra steel, which is expensive.

In parts of the world that experience an extreme climate, for instance, deserts or places with cold winters, the skin of a building must protect against widely varying temperatures. It is especially difficult and expensive to create and maintain comfortable conditions in tall buildings because of the vast amounts of glass on their exteriors. Vacuum-sealed double- and triple-glazing units, reflective glass, and sunshades all help to control the internal temperature. Even in temperate regions, the cost of running a skyscraper is becoming a critical issue, and architects are starting to design buildings that are more energy-efficient.

△ MENARA MESINIAGA 1993

Designed by Ken Yeang for IBM in Selangor, Malaysia, this 15-story building is a prototype for tropical skyscrapers of the future. It has become evident that glass skyscrapers, imitations of those designed for cooler climates, are unsuitable for tropical cities—they are expensive to cool and prone to condensation.

This innovative structure breaks away from the sealed environment of traditional buildings with their reliance on air conditioning. It is planned with the services, washrooms, and elevator lobbies on the hot sides and most of the glazing on the cooler north and south sides. A number of features limit heat gain: louvers shade the recessed windows that face east and west (the sides that receive the most sunlight); thickly planted "skycourts," or terraces, which spiral around the outside, provide shade as does a giant sun roof under which there is a swimming pool. This cooling system is supplemented with natural ventilation from windows and doors.

◁ NATIONAL COMMERCE BANK 1984

The windows and curved facade of Skidmore, Owings & Merrill's National Commerce Bank at Jeddah, in Saudi Arabia, are screened from direct sunlight in a dramatic fashion. A vast central atrium halfway up the building shades and filters the light inward, preventing it from falling directly on the windows. While the outside temperature can vary between 14°F (-10°C) and 150°F (66°C) or more, this design—coupled with special reflective glass, vacuum-sealed double- and triple-glazing units, and other devices—helps to minimize the heat gain by day and loss by night, and keeps the inside skin of the glass curtain wall at an even 68°F (20°C).

TRIBUNE TOWER
Chicago, U.S.A. 1925
462 feet (141 m)
The Gothic design of this building, by Raymond Hood and John Mead Howells, was chosen from more than 250 entries to a prestigious international competition.

PALACE OF CULTURE AND SCIENCE
Warsaw, Poland 1955
790 feet (241 m)
The Russian architect, Lev Rudnyev, was inspired by the Wrigley Building in Chicago. For many years this 42-story building, a gift from the Soviet Union to the Polish nation, was the tallest in Europe.

BANK OF CHINA
Hong Kong 1988
1,209 feet (369 m)
This elegantly proportioned and beautifully engineered glass tower, by I.M. Pei, is considered by many to be the best-looking modern skyscraper.

MESSETURM
Frankfurt, Germany 1990
850 feet (259 m)
Designed by the Chicago architect Helmut Jahn, the 55-story Messeturm (meaning "fair tower") is sited within Frankfurt's exhibition complex. Currently Europe's tallest building, it is decorated with red granite and has a glass pyramid point.

TRANSAMERICA PYRAMID
San Francisco, U.S.A. 1972 853 feet (260 m)
With its distinctive shape, this building rivals the Golden Gate Bridge as the symbol of San Francisco. It was designed by William Pereira to resist earthquakes.

HONGKONG BANK
Hong Kong, 1986 586 feet (179 m)
Acclaimed as a technological masterpiece, Norman Foster's structure seems more like a bridge than a building.

PPG PLACE
Pittsburgh, U.S.A. 1984 635 feet (194 m)
Philip Johnson created this 40-story glass fantasy as the headquarters of the Pittsburgh Plate Glass Company.

CENTRAL PLAZA
Hong Kong 1992
1,227 feet (374 m)
Asia's tallest building was designed by Ng Chun Man and Associates. It has a gold and silver glazed facade. At night it is lit by a series of vertical strips running up each face that have been aptly nicknamed "the cat scratch".

FIRST INTERSTATE BANK WORLD CENTER
Los Angeles, U.S.A. 1989
1,018 feet (310 m)
Pei Cobb Freed's 73-story steel and concrete structure has a distinctive coronet shape. It is the tallest building in the western United States.

ONE CANADA SQUARE
London, England 1991
800 feet (244 m)
Part of the ambitious Canary Wharf development, Cesar Pelli's 50-story tower dominates the London skyline. It is the tallest building in Europe after the Messeturm in Frankfurt.

CARLTON CENTRE
Johannesburg, South Africa 1973
722 feet (220 m)
With its distinctive repeating horizontal bands, this concrete-framed structure is the tallest building in Africa.

SEARS TOWER
Chicago, U.S.A. 1974
1,454 feet (443 m)
Although soon to be overtaken by Petronas Towers in Kuala Lumpur, the Sears Tower is the tallest building in the world.

FLATIRON BUILDING
New York, U.S.A. 1903
285 feet (87 m)
The triangular shape of Daniel Burnham's Flatiron makes it one of New York's best-loved buildings. It is a fine example of early eclectic skyscraper design.

WORLD TRADE CENTER
New York, U.S.A. 1972
1,368 feet (417 m)
Dominating the Manhattan waterfront, Minoru Yamasaki's somewhat featureless towers are New York's tallest skyscrapers, and are ranked second in the world after the Sears Tower.

CHRYSLER BUILDING
New York, U.S.A. 1930
1,046 feet (319 m)
Still ranked among the
10 tallest skyscrapers in
the world, the Chrysler
Building is the finest
skyscraper of the Art
Deco period. Its spire
is based on the hubcap
of Chrysler cars.

EMPIRE STATE BUILDING
New York, U.S.A. 1931
1,250 feet (381 m)
The tallest building in
the world for more
than 40 years, it
probably remains the
most celebrated.

LANDMARK TOWER
Yokohama, Japan 1993
971 feet (296 m)
Japan's tallest building is a mixed-use
development including 52 stories of
offices and a 15-story, 600-bed hotel.

SEAGRAM BUILDING
New York, U.S.A. 1958
525 feet (160 m)
The finest example of the glass
box, or International Style,
skyscraper. It was designed by
Ludwig Mies van der Rohe,
the guru of the style, with the
assistance of Philip Johnson.

WOOLWORTH BUILDING
New York, U.S.A. 1913 792 feet (241 m)
The greatest skyscraper of the eclectic
period, Cass Gilbert's beautiful Gothic
structure was the world's tallest building
for nearly 20 years.

REPUBLIC BANK CENTER
Houston, U.S.A. 1984
780 feet (238 m)
This cathedral-like building
is clad entirely in glass.
It is one of a number of
Postmodern buildings
designed by Philip Johnson.

OUB BUILDING
Singapore 1986
919 feet (280 m)
Singapore's tallest building
rises 60 stories above
Raffles Place. Designed by
Kenzo Tange, its tower is
formed from two triangles,
and its aluminium facade is
broken up by banks of
reflective glass panels.

RIALTO CENTER
Melbourne, Australia 1985
794 feet (242 m)
This 60-story reinforced
concrete office building was
designed by Gerard de Preu
and Partners. It is the tallest
building in Australia.

RELIANCE BUILDING
Chicago, U.S.A. 1895
200 feet (61 m)
One of the first skyscrapers,
Daniel Burnham's building
made full use of the newly
developed steel frame. Its
broad bay windows,
attractive terracotta facade
and narrow piers made it the
forerunner of many modern
high-rise buildings.

PETRONAS TOWERS
Kuala Lumpur, Malaysia
(under construction)
1,476 feet (450 m)
When completed,
probably in 1997, the
twin minarets of Cesar
Pelli's skyscraper will be
higher than the Sears
Tower. This will make
Petronas Towers the
world's tallest building,
taking the title away
from the United States
for the first time.

CITICORP CENTER
New York, U.S.A. 1977
919 feet (280 m)
One of the first "social
skyscrapers", Hugh
Stubbins's white building
includes a shopping
center, terraced garden
and plaza open to all.

JOHN HANCOCK CENTER
Chicago, U.S.A. 1969
1,127 feet (344 m)
"Big John", as Fazlur
Khan's tower is known,
is the tallest mixed-use
building in the world,
incorporating shops,
offices and apartments.

311 SOUTH WACKER DRIVE
Chicago, U.S.A. 1990 971 feet (296 m)
This 65-story concrete building sits next to
the Sears Tower. Designed by Kohn, Pedersen,
Fox, it consists of an octagonal tower topped
with a large glass crown that is lit up at night.

◁ **UNITED NATIONS PLAZA 1976**
*Kevin Roche, from the firm of Roche
and Dinkeloo, designed this masterful
hotel and office complex for United
Nations staff and visitors. It is
a stunning abstraction of the
International Style and one of the
most attractive postwar towers.
The blue-green reflective glass wraps
the building in a seamless curtain
which hides the steel frame and
even the divisions between floors.*

▷ **CITICORP CENTER 1977**
*The direction of tall-building design
in the 1980s was determined by the
Citicorp Center, which encapsulates
the best ideas behind the social
skyscraper. Clad in white aluminum,
it was designed by Hugh Stubbins
and engineered by Le Messurier
Consultants.*

*The complex is devoted to public
use at street level and includes
restaurants and department stores
around an atrium. Outside, around
the giant columns that support the
tower, is a plaza which includes a
sunken terrace garden and St. Peter's
Lutheran Church.*

*Citicorp's distinctive top
incorporates a remarkable piece
of engineering, known as a tuned
mass damper. It is a 400-ton block of
concrete that moves on a thin layer
of oil and is hydraulically activated to
limit the sway of the building during
high winds.*

THE SOCIAL SKYSCRAPER

**A prolonged period of experimentation began in the 1970s
as architects searched for and refined the imagery, style,
and social character of tall buildings. Skyscrapers could no
longer exist as isolated towers, each one cut off from the
street and community of which it was a part. No longer
were these buildings created just to affect the skyline; they
had to include a human face and work on a personal scale. The designs
that emerged were the forerunners of the Postmodern and Romantic
Modern skyscrapers of the late 20th century.**

**Although the John Hancock Center in Chicago was a successful mixed-
use skyscraper, it had never really interacted with its environment. The
first true social skyscrapers were the Citicorp Center and Pennzoil Place.**

The quest for a new way forward

A search for a new style of tall buildings followed the rejection of
the glass-box skyscrapers. Height was not considered a problem,
and some very tall structures were completed. But what was
needed was a style that would make tall buildings more appealing,
linking them to the urban landscape and making them part of
the community, without sacrificing their corporate identities.

Architects tackled this in a number of ways. Some remodeled
the glass facades, creating slender towers that reflected their
surroundings. Some looked to novelty and dramatic effects, as
with the "falling paper" shape of the Xerox Center. Others
designed mixed-use buildings that combined offices and
apartments with a communal plaza, atrium, or shopping or

△ **XEROX CENTER 1980**
Corporate image and architecture were perfectly wedded in Helmut Jahn's design for the Xerox Center. Located in the heart of Chicago's Loop, the building has a distinctive, curved white face that represents a piece of paper tumbling out of a copier. Its reinforced-concrete structure is clad in white-painted aluminum and reflective glass.

cultural center. In addition, architects were able to free themselves from some planning laws by promising to provide social amenities and public spaces within their buildings.

Icons of the age

The IDS Center in Minneapolis, designed by Philip Johnson and John Burgee and completed in 1972, included a hotel and shopping complex and was shaped like a flattened octagon with a faceted edge. Four years later, the same team completed Pennzoil Place in Houston. This building looks like two trapezoid towers cut away at an angle and joined by a greenhouse-type lobby. The best building of the period, however, was probably Hugh Stubbins's Citicorp Center in New York, which was completed in 1977.

◁ **333 WACKER DRIVE 1983**
Designed by William Pedersen, of the firm Kohn, Pedersen, Fox, this is one of the most elegant high-rise buildings in the world. Its shape follows the bend in the Chicago River, and its curved glass face reflects the sky and water. It is very much a modern building, yet does not completely reject the glass-box style.

▷ **FIRST INTERSTATE BANK TOWER 1985**
The 10-facet prism shape of this tower exploits the dramatic properties of the seamless glass wall. It was designed by Henry N. Cobb of Pei Cobb Freed & Partners. The 500,000 square feet (46,500 m²) of blue-green glass reflect the ever-changing Dallas sky.

This 60-story tower, which is surrounded by water gardens, was built as part of the Fountain Place development, which was awarded the American Institute of Architects' Honor Award in 1990. In the same year, it was also selected to represent the United States in the exhibition "The Socially Responsible Environment," which was staged in both Moscow and New York.

THE POSTMODERN PERIOD

Architecture was again at a crossroads in the 1980s. Only the clients seemed to know what they wanted— once again, they were aware of the power and romance of skyscrapers and wanted buildings that would represent them. Postmodernism, a reaction to the Modern Movement, or International Style, incorporated color, sculptured form, and decoration. But the choice of exact style was wide open, and a type of modern eclectic approach emerged.

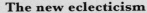

This style, which is still developing its own identity, is no longer confined to North America, with many of today's skyscrapers being built in Europe and the Far East. At present, high-rise architecture is led by Philip Johnson, William Pedersen, Cesar Pelli, and Norman Foster.

The new eclecticism

A dazzling number of styles, all loosely termed Postmodern or Romantic Modern, have been incorporated into plans for buildings since about 1980. A catalog of these styles would probably include Postmodern Classical, Polychromatic Futuristic, Engineered High Tech, Modern Expressionism, and Modern Minimalism, to name but a few. What unites most of them is the search for the symbolism that matches today's corporate culture.

As skyscraper building has spread to become a worldwide phenomenon, so the styles of architecture for tall buildings have been adapted to different cultures and climates. Whatever the country, however, the skyscraper remains primarily a method of attracting public attention and of expressing financial power.

◁ **TRUMP TOWER 1983**

Fifth Avenue glitz is epitomized by the 52-story glass tower of this retail and apartment complex, designed by Swanke, Hayden, Connell and Partners. Inside, it is embellished with bronze handrails, dazzling chandeliers, and polished pink-marble hallways.

The exterior features a series of setbacks that have been planted with trees and shrubs to create a cascading garden. But this ostentatious, rather ugly building is better seen at night, when it seems less out of place against the restrained elegance of its neighbors.

PHILIP CORTELYOU JOHNSON

The agenda for Postmodern architecture was set by Philip Johnson, who has consistently stunned, shocked, and dazzled both the public and the architectural establishment with his daring designs. Born in 1906, he has played an active part in several architectural movements. In 1932, he was appointed director of the Department of Architecture at the Museum of Modern Art in New York. It was there that he and Henry-Russell Hitchcock wrote *The International Style: Architecture Since 1922*, which described—and provided a name for—modern European architecture. More than anyone else, Johnson championed the work of Mies van der Rohe, about whom he wrote books and for whom he finally worked on the Seagram Building.

In the 1940s, Johnson set up a practice designing private houses. His own Glass House in New Canaan, Connecticut, was the first all-glass residence and a milestone in American International Style. In 1964, he teamed up with Richard Foster to design theaters and museums, but three years later left to go into partnership with John Burgee. Between 1967 and 1987, they devised some of the most stunning buildings of the Postmodern era, with clients ranging from major corporations to Shimon Perez, the Israeli prime minister, for whom they designed a nuclear bunker.

Their work included innovative social skyscrapers, such as Pennzoil Place in Houston. In 1978, however, the plans for the first truly Postmodern skyscraper, the AT&T Building in New York, were made public. It featured a roof shaped like a Chippendale cabinet and became an overnight sensation. Not everyone liked it, but they talked about it, photographed it, and wrote about it—just what the owners had wanted. Other commissions followed, including Johnson's Gothic pastiche, the Republic Bank Center in Houston and PPG Place, a glass fantasy based on London's Houses of Parliament.

In 1992, aged 84, Johnson set up a new practice, Philip Johnson Architects, working for clients such as Donald Trump.

▷ **REPUBLIC BANK CENTER 1984**
The phrase "Cathedral of Commerce" comes instantly to mind with this fantastic tower. Unashamedly showy, the 56-story building is the epitome of Postmodernism, with its spires and cascading granite and glass panels, and its sleek lines and crisp detailing.

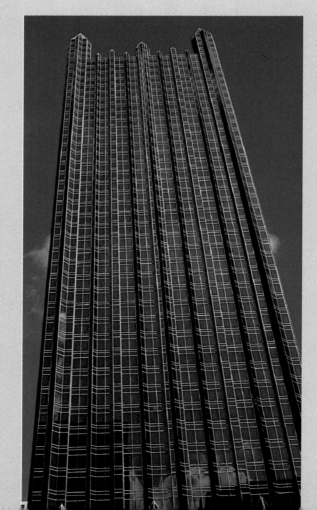

◁ **PPG PLACE 1984**
Inspired by the Victoria Tower of the Houses of Parliament in London, Philip Johnson designed a Gothic glass tower for the Pittsburgh Plate Glass Company. Although at just 635 feet (194 m) it is not very tall, its outrageous design and novelty value make it a landmark on the Pittsburgh waterfront and something of a tourist attraction.

△ AT&T BUILDING 1985

When Johnson's design for the new AT&T
(American Telephone and Telegraph)
Company skyscraper was announced in
1978, it caused great controversy and
sparked a renewed interest in architecture
from all parts of society. Paul Gapp of the
Chicago Tribune, for example, was moved
to write that "If Mies van der Rohe were
alive today, he would regard this design
with nothing less than loathing."

The top of the 37-story pinkish-granite
building (right) resembles a break-arch
pediment of the type found on Chippendale
furniture. Yet despite this strange top, the
AT&T building did not look out of place. Indeed, the pediment is only
really visible from the tops of nearby buildings, certainly not from the
street below. Furthermore, the building's Renaissance-inspired base,
with its huge arched entrance, and its clean upper-story lines put the
romance back into the skyscraper.

◁ **ONE CANADA SQUARE 1991**
Centerpiece of the Canary Wharf development—one of the biggest financial flops in history—this square stainless-steel tower has a pyramid-shaped roof. It towers over the Docklands area of London and is the second tallest building in Europe after the Messeturm in Frankfurt.

The architect, Cesar Pelli, wanted to design a building in as simple and pure a manner as possible, using a shape that was familiar to every culture.

▷ **DG BANK 1993**
Widely regarded as one of Europe's finest high-rise office buildings, this superbly proportioned skyscraper represents a new direction for architect William Pedersen.

The 682-foot (208-m) high DG Bank, with its facade of pale, finely textured granite and beautifully finished glass, is topped with a distinctive cantilevered crown. The various setbacks and divisions on its east and west sides complement the Frankfurt skyline around it.

▷ **HOTEL VILLA OLYMPICA 1990**
Spain's tallest building, this 44-story structure was commissioned as part of the stadium development for the 1992 Olympic Games in Barcelona. It was designed by Skidmore, Owings & Merrill and includes a 453-room hotel, 33 luxury apartments, and 6 floors of office space. The cross-braced exterior frame stands nearly 5 feet (1.5 m) away from the tinted glass facade and provides the architectural focus of the building.

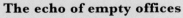

The echo of empty offices

A recession in the West, coupled with the vast business developments of the late 1980s and early 1990s, has meant that much new office space remains empty. Today, more than 20 percent of the office space in downtown Chicago is unoccupied. This surplus is enough to fulfill demand for another decade, and some of the world's biggest buildings have now also become the world's biggest financial disasters. No slick marketing can hide the fact that the business world has drastically shrunk in size.

In the struggle to survive, top architects have taken their vision and drawing boards to the growing markets of the Pacific Rim, perhaps with a stopover in Germany. For a while, London seemed to have a glowing future with its ambitious Docklands regeneration project. But the Canary Wharf project, the biggest single development ever, flopped when it was only half completed and bankrupted one of the world's biggest developers, Olympia and York, as well as countless investors and contractors.

The future of the skyscraper

In the United States, there is talk of Donald Trump and others gearing up for development again. Certainly in Asia Pacific, many new, and very tall, skyscrapers are being planned and built. In the West, skyscrapers will remain a feature of the urban skyline and, since the romance and power of tall buildings always seems to resurface, they will no doubt be joined by new examples in the future, although they may never be as tall again.

THE PACIFIC RIM CHALLENGE

Every day, the noon gun fired on the waterfront of Causeway Bay marks the passing of another 24 hours of nonstop business in Hong Kong, the city of enterprise, of noise, of the fast buck, of overcrowding—and increasingly of the skyscraper.

Hong Kong is a giant high-rise development, with more tenement buildings, luxury apartments, hotels, and commercial buildings packed into one square mile than are found in New York and Chicago put together. Looming over the Central district waterfront, in the financial heart of Hong Kong Island, stand some of the tallest buildings in the world. To the east, Central Plaza's gold and silver facade stares out over the Kowloon hillside to mainland China, while the smooth sail of I.M. Pei's Bank of China tower watches over Victoria Harbour. These two rank as the fourth and fifth highest finished buildings in the world. Central Plaza, at 1,227 feet (374 m), is also the world's tallest reinforced concrete building.

But they may not hold these positions for long, since some of the world's fastest-growing economies are to be found in Southeast Asia and China, and this region is the birthplace of a new generation of supertall buildings. China, Malaysia, Taiwan, and other ambitious countries are commissioning megastructures to signal their arrival on the international scene and their ability to compete with the more established markets of Hong Kong, Singapore, and Japan. As a result, the cities of the Pacific Rim will soon overtake New York and Chicago as leaders in the field of the tall building.

So far, the oil-rich Malaysians are in the lead, with Cesar Pelli's Petronas Towers in Kuala Lumpur. It is set in a prime 100-acre (40-ha) site of unspoilt greenery, which was previously the Selangor Turf Club. Foundations for the towers, which will resemble minarets, are complete, and handover of what will be the world's tallest building is scheduled for early 1997.

A short distance to the east of Petronas Towers, another, smaller skyscraper is under construction. The 722-foot (220-m) high Ampung Tower, designed by Kevin Roche, of the firm Roche and Dinkeloo, is due to be finished at about the same time. The majority of the next generation of skyscrapers will be built in the Far East, although some tall buildings are still being planned in the West.

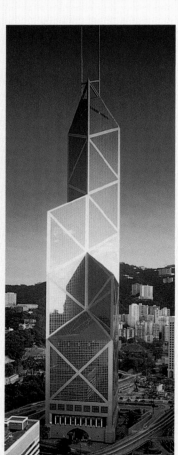

△ **BANK OF CHINA 1988**
The sight of I.M. Pei's 1,209-foot (369-m) blue-gray streamlined tower brings gasps of awe and wonder at the smoothness of its composition and the elegance of the external bracing, set off by the glass and aluminum curtain wall. Built for the Bank of China in Hong Kong, it is a masterpiece of both modern architecture and structural engineering.

▷ **CENTRAL PLAZA**
1992
Something of an Empire State Building lookalike, this gleaming 1,227-foot (374-m) high tower is wrapped in a silver and gold glass jacket. It is equally dazzling at night, with its lines of colored neon, "the cat scratch," running the length of the building.

◁ **LANDMARK TOWER**
1993
The forceful, muscular, but elegantly tapering Landmark Tower on the harbor front in Yokohama is set against the heavenly backdrop of Mount Fujiyama. This 73-story, 971-foot (296-m) granite-clad building, the tallest in Japan, was designed by Stubbins Associates as a mixed-use development. It includes 52 floors of offices and, above them, 15 floors of hotel accommodation.

▷ **PETRONAS TOWERS**
As this artist's impression shows, Cesar Pelli's design was inspired by Islamic architecture and symbolism. This mighty monument, expected to be finished in 1997, is set in a 100-acre (40-hectare) site of unspoilt greenery in Kuala Lumpur, the capital of Malaysia. When completed, the minarets, which are joined by a sky bridge at the 25th floor, will rise to 1,476 feet (450 m)— 22 feet (7m) higher than the Sears Tower—making Petronas Towers the world's tallest building.

Shanghai in its heyday, in the early 1900s, was the enterprise capital of the Far East. This position gradually diminished and was finally lost with the Japanese invasion of 1937 and the subsequent communist regime. This caused millions of refugees, and billions in hard currency, to transfer to nearby Hong Kong.

The recent liberalization of communism in China has, however, rekindled the flame of enterprise, and in the Pudong district of Shanghai—an agricultural and industrial backwater—the stage is being set for a comeback. Shacks have been cleared and fields drained to make way for the glistening 1,381-foot (421-m) Jin Mao tower, designed by Skidmore, Owings & Merrill. Elsewhere in China, other skyscrapers are being planned. Some 800 miles (1,300 km) west of Shanghai in Chongqing, the capital of Sichuan province, another skyscraper is under construction, which, at 1,500 feet (457 m), will become the tallest in the world when completed.

Although some notable projects, such as La Tour Sans Fins (tower without end) in Paris, are being planned in the West, the focus of the financial and business world is shifting inexorably to the East. And it is clear that, in the eyes of the Asians, the acquisition of a skyscraper can enable a nation to leapfrog from Third World to First World ranking overnight. To this end, they commission tall, visually imposing buildings. And China is not the only country where this is happening; throughout the Far East, new supertall buildings are being designed and constructed.

The mix of Western architecture with Eastern money and values is proving interesting. But it remains to be seen whether a skyscraper standing among the rice fields will bring the expected prosperity, and whether the vast Millennium Tower being planned by the Japanese, to re-exert their superiority over the region, will really be the answer to their overcrowding problem.

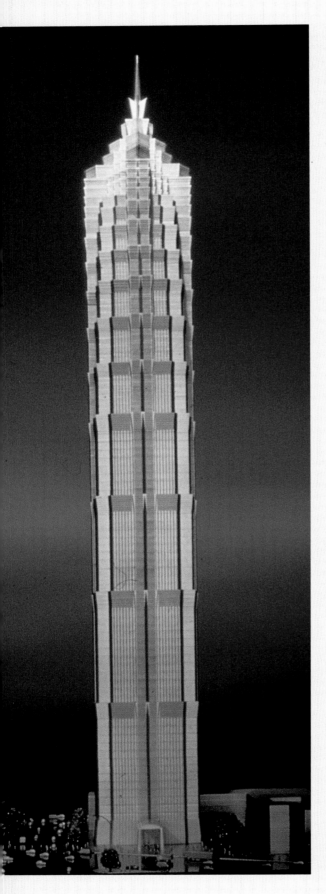

◁ **JIN MAO**
East meets West in this pagoda fantasy by the Chicago firm of Skidmore, Owings & Merrill for the China Shanghai Foreign Trade Company. The plan of Jin Mao is based on the lucky number eight to give it good **feng shui**, or harmony—its setbacks are arranged in multiples of eight. When it is finished, this office and hotel complex will have 88 stories, for double good fortune.

▽ **CHONGQING TOWER**
This model shows the 1,500-foot (457-m) high tower being built at Chongqing, China. It was designed by the New York firm of Haines, Lundberg, Waehler as a 114-story framed tube structure clad in glass and metal. Toward the top, the faceted facade is broken by an eight-story atrium giving views over the surrounding landscape.

▷ **MILLENNIUM TOWER**
A vertical city in which 50,000 people can live, work, and relax, this conical tower is an idea for the 21st century. Designed for the Obayashi Corporation in Tokyo by Sir Norman Foster and Partners, it incorporates a helical steel construction, woven like a basket. This gives an immensely strong, yet lightweight, structure which would support the great height of 2,755 feet (840 m)—almost twice that of the Sears Tower.

High-speed elevators would whisk people up to "sky centers" at every 30th floor, with meeting points, gardens, stores, and food halls. Even if this design is not realized, it points to towers of the future.

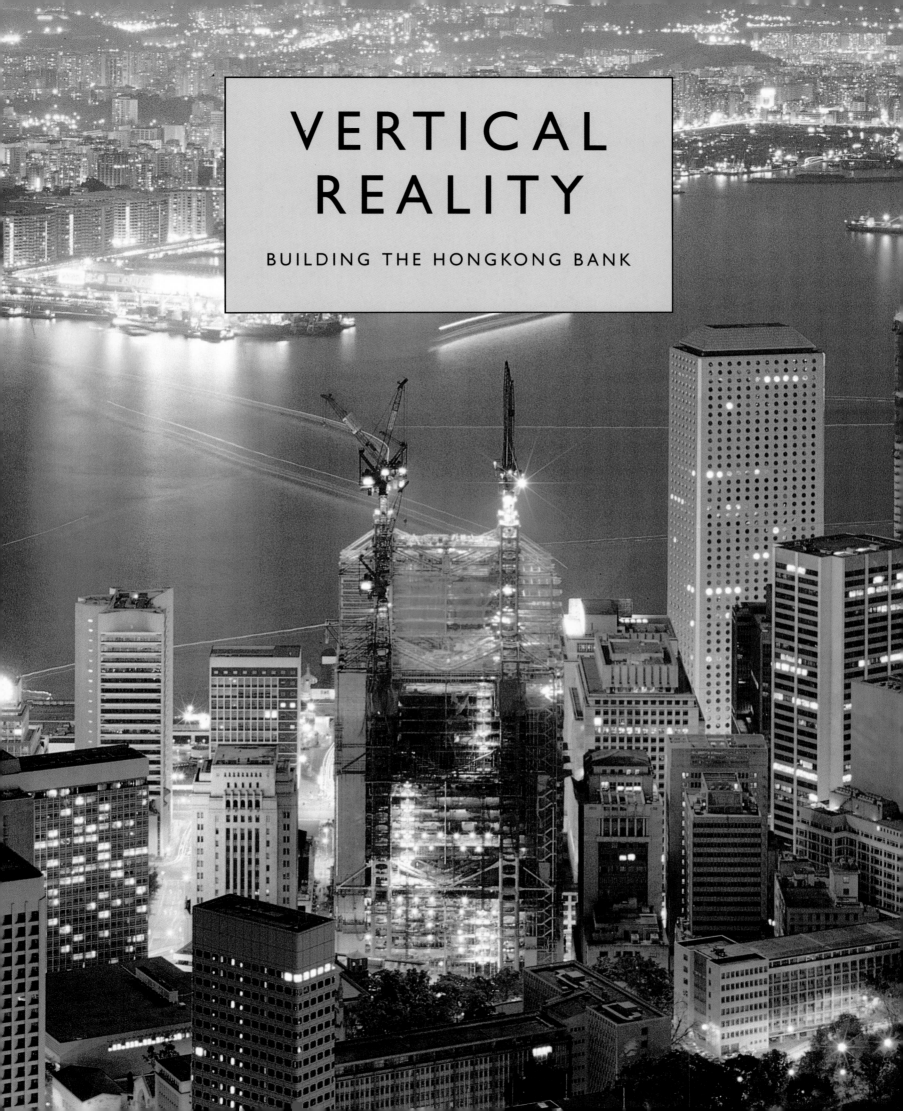

VERTICAL
REALITY

BUILDING THE HONGKONG BANK

In 1978, the board of the Hongkong & Shanghai Bank (now known as the Hongkong Bank) decided to replace their old headquarters, which had been completed in 1935, with a new building. Since the end of World War II, the Bank had expanded its operations into more than 50

Old building shown on a bill

countries and had risen through the rankings to become the 14th largest bank in the world. This expansion had far outstripped the capacity of the old headquarters building, and many departments were scattered around Hong.Kong.

With the changes in information technology, the speed of modern banking business, and the enormous growth of funds and operations, the Bank, according to its chairman Michael Sandberg, had become "like a suit which one could no longer fit into." It was, however, a momentous decision to demolish a building that was more than just a much-loved landmark, it was a symbol of stability and prosperity

Norman Foster

for both the Bank and the colony. There was a real fear among the superstitious that such an act could spell disaster not only for the Bank's profitability, but also for its position as one of the most powerful banking corporations in the Far East.

Once committed to a new building, the board wanted to make sure that

its design would be imaginative and yet still give the institution the same presence and visibility that had been such a bonus with the old building. They drew up a shortlist of seven internationally known architectural firms which were invited to "submit proposals for the best bank in the world." The final choice, the English architect Norman Foster, seemed rather surprising since he had never built a bank, had never designed a skyscraper, and had no experience of working in Hong Kong.

This is the story of the design and construction of Foster's bank—one of the most original, most thought-provoking, and most expensive skyscrapers ever built.

COMPETITION PLAN

AT THE INITIAL COMPETITION BRIEFING, the seven architects chosen by the Bank were told to look at two possibilities that would allow the Bank to operate during construction: partial redevelopment of the site, retaining the North Tower and banking hall; and a phased redevelopment plan. The lack of alternative space in central Hong Kong ruled out total demolition and a new start. Sir Norman Foster and Partners developed a design strategy which it

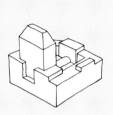
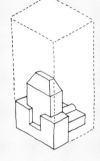

called phased regeneration, with the emphasis on giving the clients as many development options as possible.

The team built up a picture of the way in which the building was to be used, by interviewing banking staff at all levels. Foster himself spent nearly three weeks in Hong Kong—sketching ideas and meeting people—captivated by the vibrancy and dynamism of the place. He wanted his building to reflect the essence of Hong Kong and its culture. And although the building would be a high rise, it had to maintain a human scale.

His idea was to build a new structure over the existing banking hall, which could, if necessary, be expanded to cover the whole site. This ingeniously simple idea led to a design that resembled a multistory extendible bridge. Five concrete towers on each side supported the structure, with the floors suspended from huge trusses set at three points up the building. The services were placed on the ends of the building, beside the towers, so they could be replaced easily and would not block out the light or the spectacular views.

◁ *This early sketch by Norman Foster shows the bridgelike suspension structure. In essence, this design is very close to that of the building as it was finally built.*

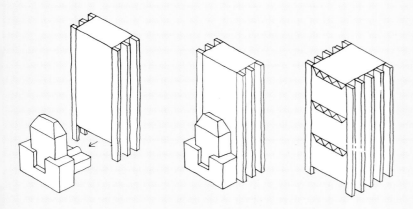

△ *Minimal disruption was the object behind Foster's concept of "phased regeneration." By designing a structure that was suspended rather like a bridge, he allowed the Bank time to decide, almost as construction progressed, whether to retain the North Tower and the old banking hall, with its famous painted ceiling, or whether to demolish everything and have an entirely new building.*

The sequence of sketches (above) illustrates the concept. The first two show the old building and the maximum volume of the site. Next, the North Tower and banking hall remain, and the first phase of the new structure—three towers on each side—is built. The final sketch—with all the phases complete— shows a totally new building made up of five towers.

Models were made to demonstrate the principles involved. Before the presentation to the board, the fourth stage of the sequence was assembled on the balcony of Foster's hotel room (above right), with the existing 1935 building in the background.

▷ *Although the idea of retaining the existing structure had inspired this design, the plans and models presented to the board showed a complete new building. The gaps between the trusses and the floor above show the floors to be suspended and not supported from below. The idea of the banking hall as an atrium, reached by escalators, was a feature of this scheme.*

△ *Foster recognized the symbolic importance of color in traditional Chinese architecture. Since red was often used for important public buildings, it was incorporated into the chevron plan (above).*

DESIGN DEVELOPMENTS

ONCE FOSTER HAD WON THE COMPETITION and been chosen as the architect, the board abandoned the idea of retaining any of the old building, since it would preclude the use of deep basements for storage vaults and plant rooms. Foster's design had developed from an awareness of the Bank's need for flexibility and a variety of building options, both before and during construction. Therefore, the decision to rebuild from scratch did not seem, at the time, to herald a fundamental design rethink.

Chevron plan

After nearly a year, the chevron plan was presented. In essence, this structure allowed almost unlimited spatial flexibility. The heavy trusses and massive concrete supports of the competition entry were replaced by a delicate lattice of V-shaped steelwork and slimline masts. The interior could be arranged in a myriad of ways. Parts of floors could be left open to the air or landscaped as "gardens in the sky," but they could easily be converted into offices should the need arise.

When the plan was finally presented, there were problems. The Chinese board members were immediately worried about the *feng shui* aspect of the building. They felt that the downward thrust of the chevrons could symbolize money and prestige going down the drain. The subsequent rejection of the scheme came as a complete surprise to Foster who, only weeks before, had shown his ideas to a delighted chairman. But the chairman was not Chinese and did not have the same faith in *feng shui*.

Organ pipe plan

The rejection of the chevron plan led to a complete change of direction in the design. The bridgelike structure was abandoned and a totally new

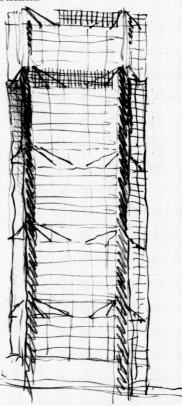

△ *The coat hanger plan, as the design that emerged from this sketch became known, was the breakthrough that harmonized the structural form with the architectural concept of the competition entry. Note the open plaza at the base, the setback at the fourth trusses, and the truss diagonals.*

look explored. The organ pipe plan was based on a mass of more conventional towers. Inspired by regulations about the shadows thrown by tall buildings, it took the form of a group of blocks with setbacks at different levels. This design was unpopular and was never fully developed, although some models were made. Experimenting with this design was positive, however, since it helped to develop the idea of setbacks.

Coat hanger plan

The final alternative, the so-called coat hanger plan, was the breakthrough that finally combined the structure of the competition scheme with the setbacks of the organ pipe plan. Here the trusses of the competition plan return as double-height suspension bridges, known as coat hangers in Foster's office. The idea of a central atrium was revived and expanded, and an open plaza area was left at the base. Many aspects of this plan were extremely close to what was eventually decided upon and built.

◁ *The organ pipe plan, as this design was nicknamed, was a radical departure from Foster's previous ideas. It resembled a cluster of kaboblike towers. This created a structure with terraces that could be set back in any direction, thus minimizing the shadow line. Its massive form, however, did not appeal to the Bank.*

FENG SHUI

Literally translated as "wind and water," feng shui *is the ancient Chinese system of divination aimed at harmonizing the human landscape with the natural world. The direction in which a building faces, the position of mountains, rivers, roads, trees, and the prevailing winds all affect the* feng shui *aspects of a site.*

Foster and his associates regularly consulted the Bank's geomancer, Koo Pak Ling, to make sure that no principles of feng shui *were violated during the planning, construction, and fitting out of the building. Koo Pak Ling's sketch (right) identified the best corner of entry to the new building and thus the most auspicious position for the main escalators. He advised that these escalators should be aligned with the tail of a dragon whose shadow fell from a nearby peak.*

Before the Bank's two bronze guardian lions were moved from the old building to their temporary resting place in Statue Square, Koo Pak Ling, with the help of special feng shui *cards, decided on the most propitious time. At 4 A.M. one Sunday, he supervised the movement of the lions, making sure that they were lowered simultaneously by two cranes to avoid showing favor.*

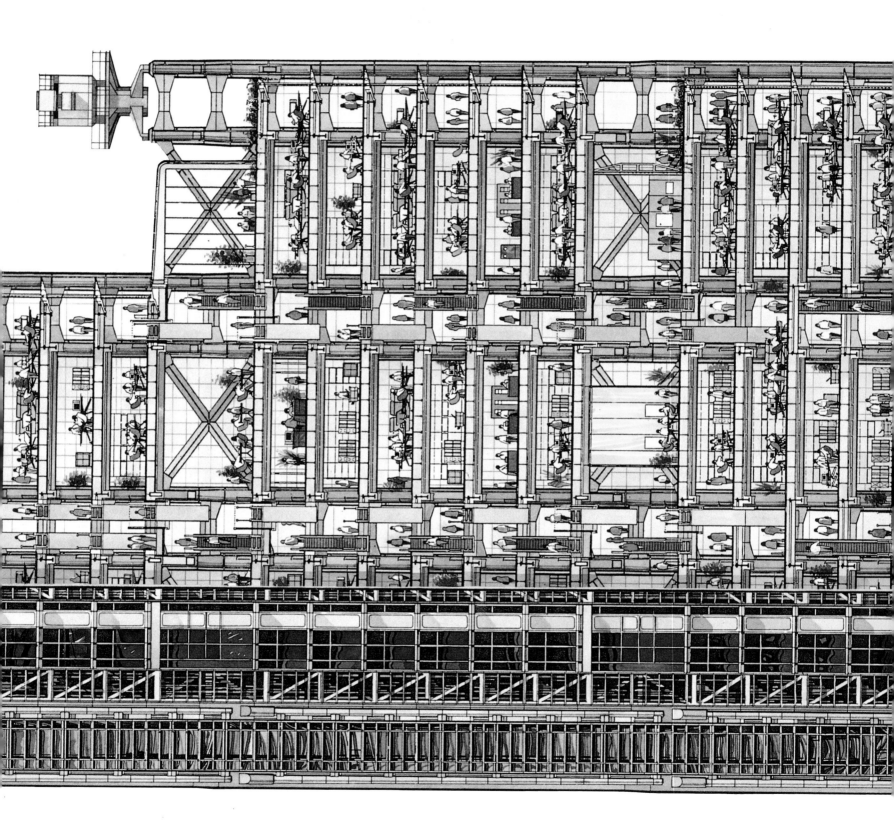

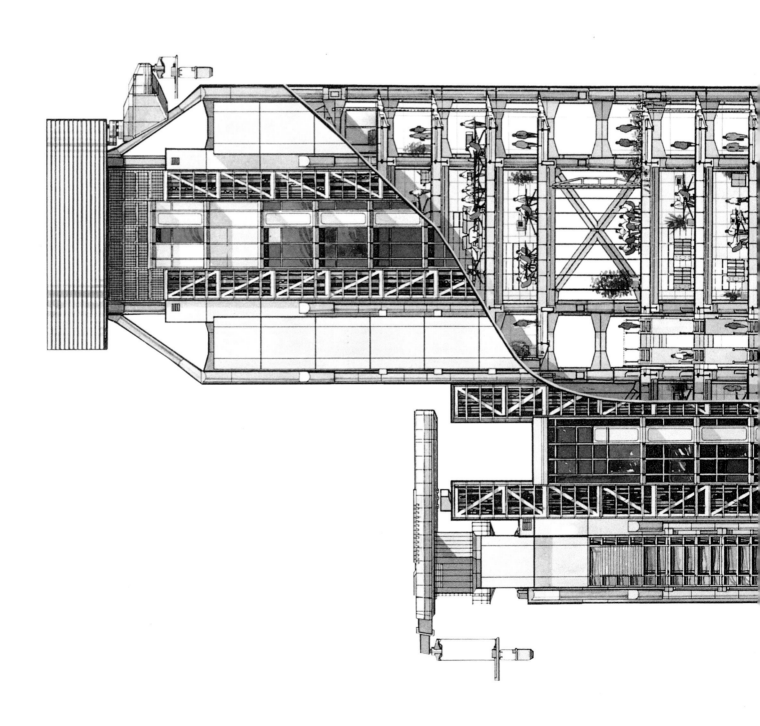

Viewing gallery
Level 44

Directly beneath the gray panels on the top of the building is the viewing gallery. Glazed on all sides, it gives spectacular panoramic views of Hong Kong. Below, at level 41, the executive reception suite opens out onto a rooftop patio garden.

Boardroom Level 35/36

At the level of the fourth suspension truss, this room is entered through double-height doors and is dominated by the huge mahogany table with ebony inlay. The acoustics are enhanced by microphones built into the table which are connected to small loudspeakers set in the oval "chandelier."

Elevator lobby

Levels 11, 20, 28, 33, 41

Express elevators go directly to each lobby located at a suspension truss. From there, people take escalators to their own floors.

This system is both efficient and more personal because it allows for more human interaction.

North–south section

- 47 Roof
- 46 Plant room
- 45 Plant room

- 44 Viewing gallery
- 43 Private dining rooms
- 41/42 Elevator lobby, executive reception suite, terrace
- 40 Chairman's apartment
- 39
- 38
- 37
- 35/36 Elevator lobby, boardroom, conference facilities, terrace
- 34 Executive offices and reception
- 33
- 32 Maintenance crane
- 31
- 30

Maintenance crane

- 28/29 Elevator lobby and executive dining terrace
- 27 Main kitchens
- 26
- 25
- 24
- 23
- 22
- 20/21 Elevator lobby and staff terrace
- 19
- 18
- 17
- 16

Executive reception suite Level 41/42

At the level of the fifth suspension truss, the executive reception suite, which can only be reached by private elevator, gives access to private dining rooms, the viewing gallery, and the patio garden.

Through the glass wall, a double-height cross brace can be seen between the tops of two masts. Each of these masts supports a maintenance crane.

Maintenance cranes

Levels 30, 37, 43, 45

Installed for window cleaning and attending to repairs to the exterior, the maintenance cranes are clad to match the rest of the building.

Main dining area Level 28/29

This double-height area acts both as a dining room and as the main meeting place for the building. Food is prepared in the kitchens, one floor below, and brought up by elevator. Small mezzanine balconies are formed at the interchange of the escalators going to level 30.

Atrium   Levels 3–12

Separated from the plaza by a glazed underbelly, the atrium is the centerpiece of the building. Sunlight is reflected down from the mirrors of the internal sunscoop into the space below. Banks of glazed elevator shafts and the bridges that link the gallery floors on each side can be seen behind the giant cross brace at the "Cathedral Wall" end of the atrium.

Sunscoop   Level 12

On the south side of the building, the 480 glass mirrors of the external sunscoop gather sunlight and reflect it inside onto the 225 aluminum reflectors of the internal sunscoop at the top of the atrium.

Main banking hall   Level 3

This well-lit and spacious double-storied banking area takes the form of two galleries overlooking the atrium and plaza below. A sweep of 22 teller counters runs along each side of the hall, designed to cope with many thousands of customers each day. Because of the way the counters have been designed, there is no need for impersonal security screens.

Basement banking hall   Level B1

Just below the plaza is another banking hall where larger commercial and cash transactions are handled and a vault is needed. This area, reached via a pair of escalators from the east side of the plaza, also acts as the reception point for the main safe deposit vault on the floor below.

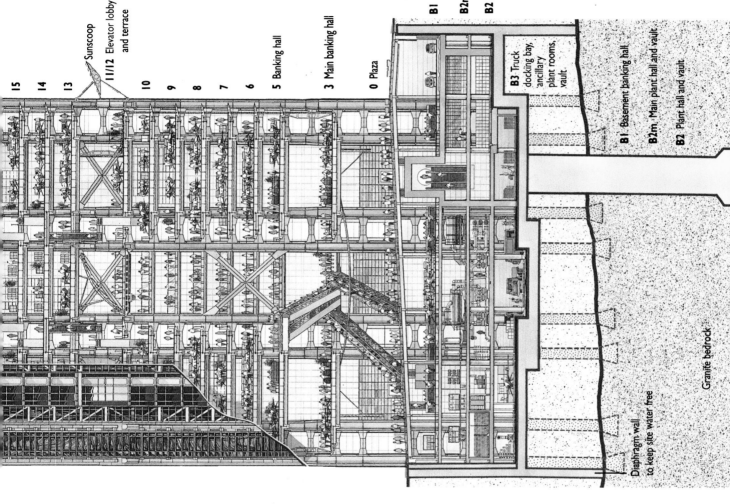

Sunscoop

11/12   Elevator lobby and terrace

15
14
13

10
9
8
7
6

5   Banking hall

3   Main banking hall

0   Plaza

B1
B2m
B2

B3   Truck docking bay, ancillary plant rooms, vault.

B1   Basement banking hall

B2m   Main plant hall and vault

B2   Plant hall and vault

Diaphragm wall to keep site water free

Granite bedrock

Seawater tunnel

Atrium   Levels 3–12

Entrance plaza   Level 0

Two escalators move people up through the glazed underbelly to the main banking hall. Escalators are more efficient than elevators at taking a steady stream of people up into the building. The plaza, guarded by the Bank's two bronze lions, is always open, although there are retractable glass screens to give typhoon protection.

Seawater tunnel

Deep underground, sea water, for use in the chillers of the air-conditioning system and as flush water for the toilets, is piped from the harbor to the Bank and back again. The supply of the sea water is handled by one pipe, the return by another, and the third is a standby.

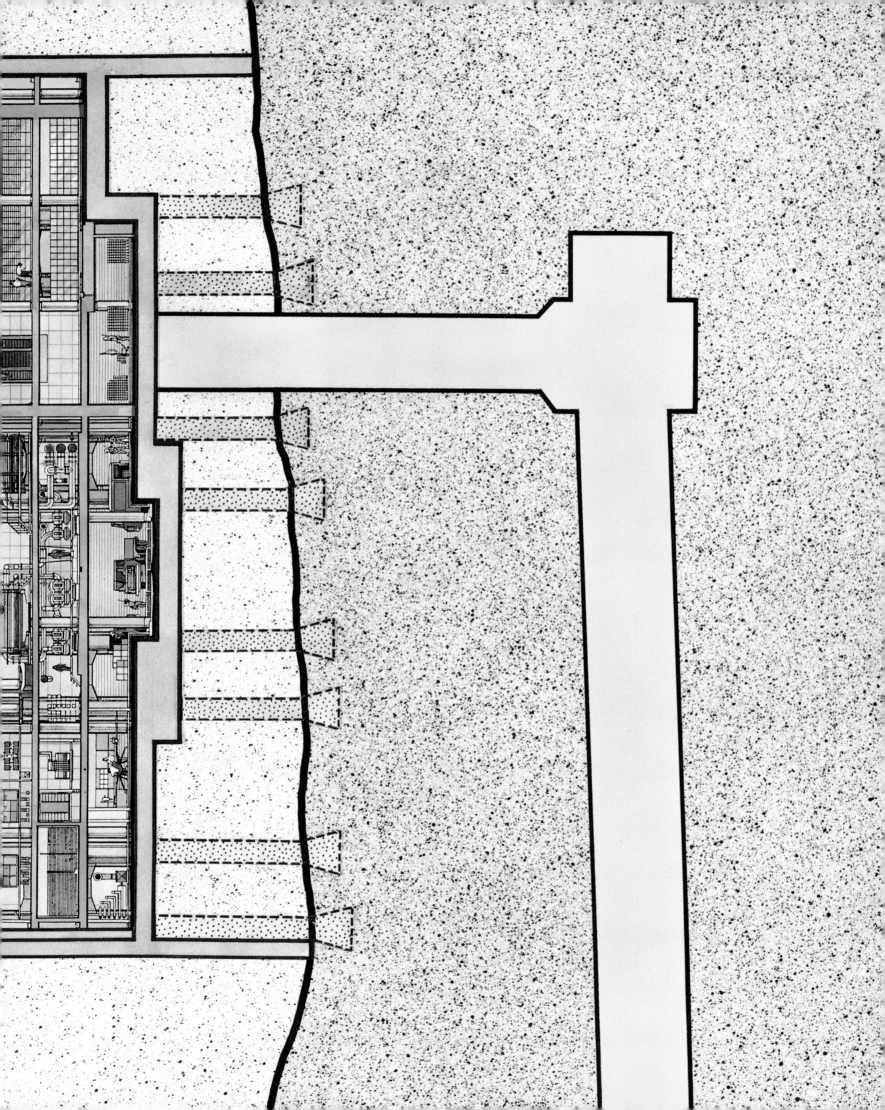

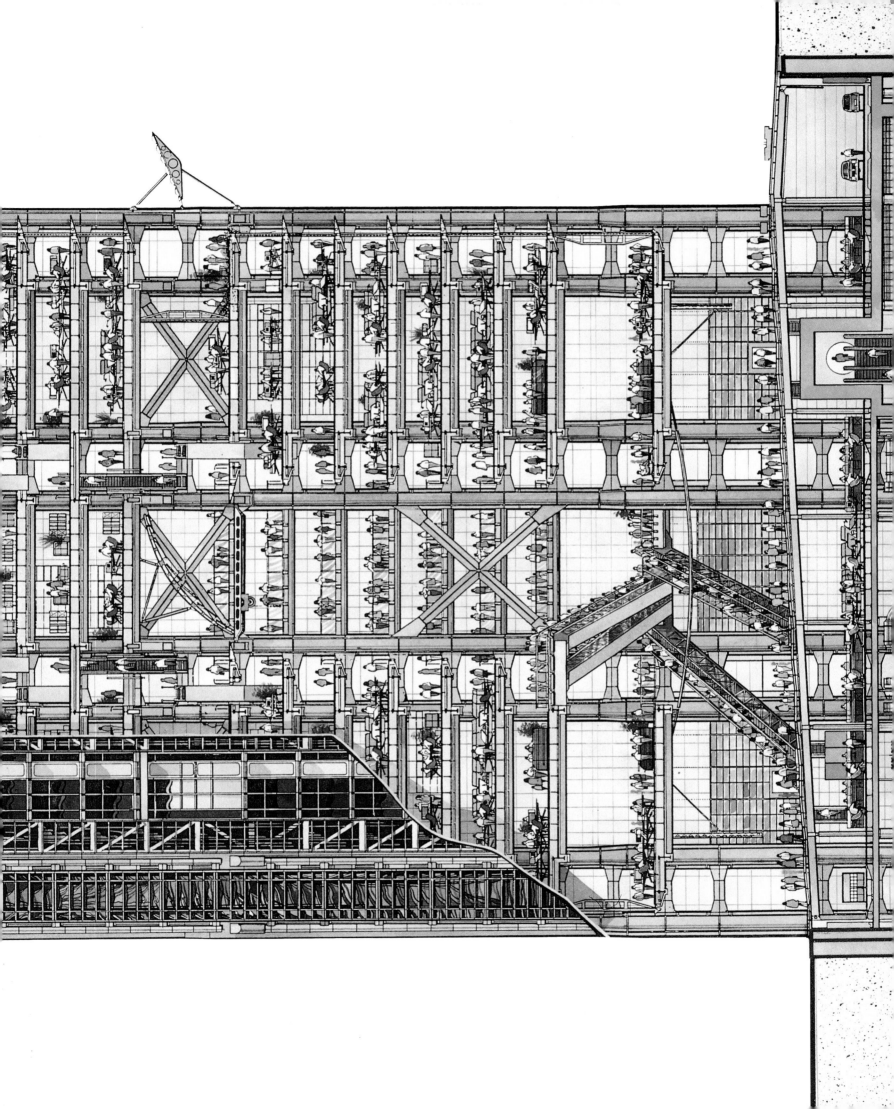

FINAL PLAN

THE DESIGN HAD COME FULL CIRCLE by January 1981, and a hybrid of the coat hanger plan was approved by the board. The huge concrete towers of the competition plan were refined to eight steel masts; and the idea of floors that hung from great trusses was retained, ensuring maximum flexibility of the internal space. The center-piece of the building was to be a 12-story atrium, as tall as the nave of Cologne Cathedral, lit using daylight reflected in from an external sunscoop.

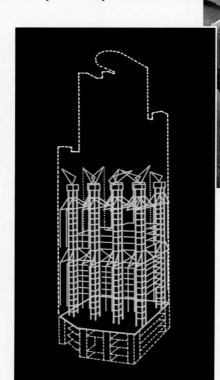

Hong Kong's strict planning regulations required that the top of the building be set back so as not to overshadow the street. Since the two rows of four masts effectively divided the building into three equal segments, this was achieved by stopping the two outer segments at the third and fourth suspension trusses, leaving just the central bay to be built close to the full height of 590 feet (180 m), the maximum allowed at the time. This restriction has since been lifted.

Once the final design had been resolved, detailed speci-fications had to be drafted and agreed. During the course of the planning and construction, more than 120,000 draw-ings were issued—sometimes at a rate of 300 a week. For the cladding alone, Sir Norman Foster and Partners produced some 2,500 working drawings.

The lack of time and space on site meant that components had to be prefabricated. This was an advantage, since build-ing components could be produced simultaneously and in a controlled environment where quality could be maintained. In all, more than 100 individual contracts were awarded to companies in 12 countries around the world. The service modules, for example, were made in Japan; the cladding and curtain walling were shipped from the United States; the steelwork came from Britain; the escalators from Germany; and the stone flooring from both Finland and Italy. Simply coordinating the arrival, storage, and assembly of everything was a logistical nightmare.

△ *Scale models, such as this 1:100 version of the final scheme (above), were made at various stages in the design process. They pinpointed problems that might only have come to light during construction and gave a fuller understanding both of the visual and technical impact of design decisions.*

Another tool used increasingly by architects and engineers is Computer-Aided Design, or CAD (left). It not only allows detailed plans to be generated, but also analyzes the stresses and movements of every element of a structure, even taking into account the settling of the foundations as the height of the building increases.

▷ *Photomontages give clients a realistic idea of what a proposed building will look like. Here, a photograph of a 1:500-scale model has been superimposed onto a picture of Hong Kong. It shows the final scheme— viewed from the northeast— towering above the old Bank of China building. Two years after the Hongkong Bank was finished, a huge new Bank of China skyscraper was built nearby.*

HOW THE BUILDING WORKS

The Hongkong Bank is designed more like a bridge than a traditional building.

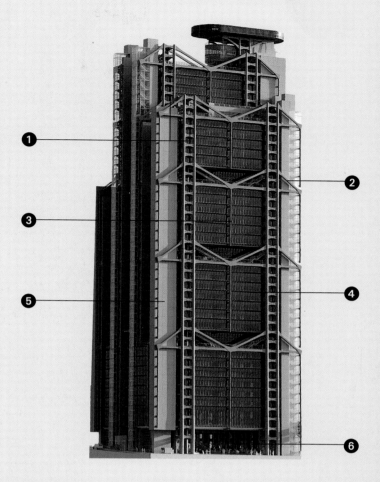

❶ The whole structure is supported by eight masts, arranged in two rows of four. Each mast is made up of four tubular steel columns, which are braced by rectangular beams, known as vierendeels, and supported on foundations driven into bedrock more than 100 feet (30 m) below ground.

❷ Suspension trusses, located at five points up the building, give the distinctive double-height "gallery zones." Two-story-high cross braces between the masts provide added stability (shown below).

❸ The floors are attached to hangers, steel tubes that are suspended from the center and ends of the truss above.

❹ Each floor consists of two parallel main beams that connect to the hangers, with interconnecting secondary beams supporting a sheet-metal deck topped with 4 inches (100 mm) of reinforced concrete.

❺ Stacks of prefabricated modules, on the east and west sides of the building, contain toilets and machinery, such as air conditioning, for each floor.

❻ The plaza at the base of the building is an extension to Statue Square, which is in front of the Bank. The plaza is open 24 hours a day, although there are retractable glass screens to provide protection against typhoons.

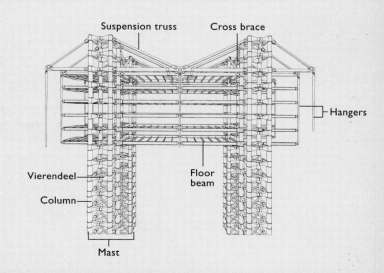

▷ **Digging the foundations by hand** was the quickest and cheapest option open to the developers. A husband and wife team of Hong Kong Chinese lived under each of the tarpaulins dotted over the site. Working 12 hours a day, 7 days a week, each team dug one of the 58 foundations. Thirty-two of these, arranged in groups of four, anchor the eight masts, while the rest support the basement floor. All the foundation work was completed in just 35 days—it would have taken four months with machines. Before digging could begin, however, dry working conditions were necessary. So a 3-foot (0.9-m) thick diaphragm wall was built around the entire site down to bedrock, and the huge "pool" of underground water that it trapped was then pumped out.

△ **Because of a shortage of time and space,** an unusual top-down construction process was used—only the foundations were excavated to start with, not the entire site. Once the foundations were completed, the masts could be assembled, and the basements dug at the same time. For each of the eight masts, a large access shaft, or caisson, 32 feet (10 m) across and 56 feet (17 m) deep, was excavated to the lowest basement level. From there, four smaller holes were dug a further 50 feet (15 m), into the granite bedrock. These deeper holes were then filled with concrete and capped to form bases (above) ready to receive the first steel mast sections.

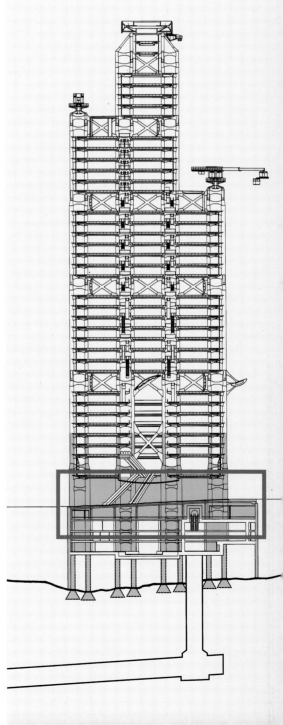

JUNE 1983

STEEL SUPERSTRUCTURE
Floor at level 3 in place; masts to level 7.

SERVICES AND CLADDING
Production of modules and cladding under way.

BASEMENTS
Floor of basement level B1 complete; excavation
under way for level B2m.

FOUNDATIONS
Diaphragm walls in place around whole site and
all caissons complete.

SEAWATER TUNNEL
Excavation began in February.

◁ *Small excavators* dug out the basements at the same time as the masts were being assembled above ground. The next job was to install steel reinforcement into which concrete was poured to cast the floor slab. Once completed, excavation of the next level down could begin. As a caisson was revealed, its outer casing was removed to expose the steel mast inside. The floor slab of the deepest basement, excavated in the fall, was 3 feet (0.9 m) thick. It was held down with rock anchors—grouted steel ties drilled into the bedrock—to resist the upward pressure of underground water.

△ *The cranes* climbed with the building. They were attached to the lower section of a mast and rose up hydraulically as mast sections were completed. After a slow start, the masts have reached level 7 (above). Before the mast sections arrived on site, they were coated with a cement-based protection against corrosion, giving them their gray color. The red sections are unprotected vierendeels and welded pieces, to be sprayed at a later date. Tents over the masts allowed welding to continue in any weather and were also used to enclose the areas of steel being sprayed on site.

▷ **Lack of site space** and construction time meant that services for individual floors were made in prefabricated modules that could be plugged into the east and west sides of the building.

IT IS PROBABLY THIS →

POSSIBLE ALSO - BUT LESS LIKELY!

Foster's concern for detail even extended to the design of the faucets on the washbasins. Drawings of each type of module were prepared by the architects in conjunction with the subcontractors, and a full-size mock-up was tested before production began.

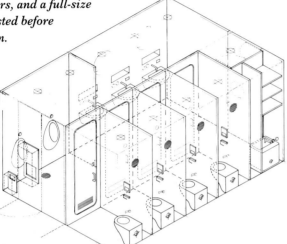

△ **Mass production** of the 139 service modules saved assembly time and guaranteed quality. The modules were built by HMT, a Japanese consortium consisting of the companies Hitachi, Mitsubishi, and Toshiba.

Most modules were designed to contain toilet facilities and local air-conditioning machinery, although some held secondary plant such as boilers, power generators, and electrical substations.

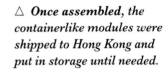

△ **Once assembled,** the containerlike modules were shipped to Hong Kong and put in storage until needed.

◁ **The first module** was hoisted into position on 12 November; only 10 months later, the final one was secured in place. Due to their size and weight, the modules had to be delivered to the site on specially modified trucks which followed a route that avoided narrow roads, traffic, and overhanging signs. To avoid congestion, all but the first module were transported at night. Once they were in position, the modules only had to be connected to the water and power supplies and, in the case of the washrooms, filled with soap, towels, and toilet paper.

SEPTEMBER–NOVEMBER 1983

STEEL SUPERSTRUCTURE
Masts in place to level 20, just below second truss.
Installation of escape staircases starts.

PROTECTION AND CLADDING
On-site spraying of corrosion protection begins.

SERVICES
First service modules installed.

BASEMENTS
Installation of plant-room pipework begins in
completed basement levels B1, B2m, and B2.
Excavation of level B3 begins.

SEAWATER TUNNEL
Excavation of main tunnel 30 percent complete.

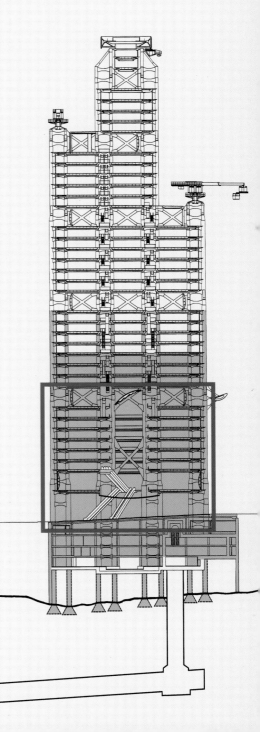

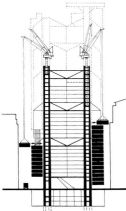

◁ **Six cranes** lifted all the modules and steelwork into position. Space restrictions dictated that the cranes were attached to the masts themselves. During the peak construction period, around August 1984, more than 300 tons of steel were delivered to the site each day.

△ **Powerful floodlights** fixed under the cranes allowed work to continue 24 hours a day. On 9 September 1983, Typhoon Ellen struck Hong Kong, causing damage and flooding, but the sails attached to the cranes had allowed them to move freely with the wind and so avoid colliding with each other. Ten days later, the steel structure was completed to the first suspension truss (above).

◁ *The impressive size of the atrium, with its galleried floors on either side, is already apparent behind the bamboo scaffolding. The three-story-high cross bracing and the support structure for the elevators are also in position in front of the so-called Cathedral Wall. An early sketch (right) shows how Foster visualized customers entering the plaza and riding up on escalators, through some kind of transparent barrier, to the double-height main banking hall. In the event, this barrier became a curved glass underbelly.*

△ *The excavation of the seawater tunnel between the Bank and the harbor is now almost complete. With a diameter of 23 feet (7 m) and a total length of 1,150 feet (350 m), the completed tunnel allows 275 gallons (1,250 liters) of sea water to circulate every second. The water acts as the coolant for the air-conditioning system and as flush water for the toilets. Although the tunnel was expensive, by saving the 25,000 square feet (2,320 m²) of space needed by a conventional air-conditioning plant, it paid for itself within 10 years.*

JANUARY 1984

STEEL SUPERSTRUCTURE
Complete to level 26. Escape staircases installed to level 15.

PROTECTION AND CLADDING
Corrosion protection to steelwork complete to level 23. First cladding panel lifted into position.

SERVICES
Modules installed to level 15. Installation of subfloor services, including telecommunication and power cables, begins.

BASEMENTS
Complete to level B2m. Waterproofing and installation of first machinery in progress. Work continues drilling rock anchors to secure level B3.

SEAWATER TUNNEL
Excavation of main tunnel complete. Tunnel shaft connected to basement level B3.

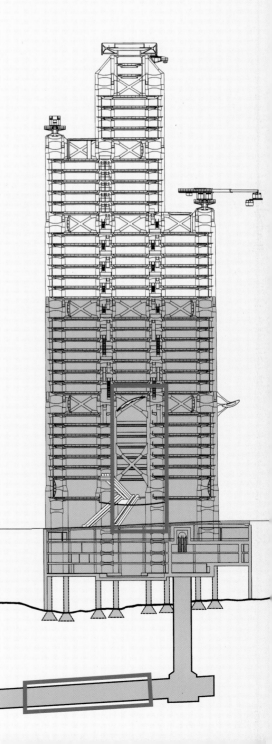

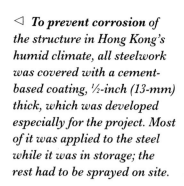

◁ **To prevent corrosion** of the structure in Hong Kong's humid climate, all steelwork was covered with a cement-based coating, ½-inch (13-mm) thick, which was developed especially for the project. Most of it was applied to the steel while it was in storage; the rest had to be sprayed on site.

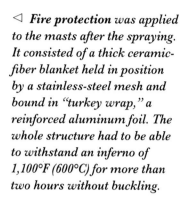

◁ **Fire protection** was applied to the masts after the spraying. It consisted of a thick ceramic-fiber blanket held in position by a stainless-steel mesh and bound in "turkey wrap," a reinforced aluminum foil. The whole structure had to be able to withstand an inferno of 1,100°F (600°C) for more than two hours without buckling.

△ **A sawn-off World War II fighter plane** and a grid of sprinklers were used to simulate the weather conditions during a Hong Kong typhoon. Full-scale prototypes for each of the main cladding elements were tested for watertightness by blasting them with wind and water at 200 mph (320 km/h).

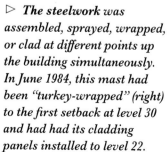

◁ **External cladding** not only gives a uniform appearance, but also protects the components from wind and rain. To achieve the smooth, non-fading finish required, the ⅕-inch (5-mm) thick aluminum panels were finished with a polymer coating that was baked on at 840°F (450°C). Every piece of cladding, whether for the masts, curtain walling, or module towers, was made to an accuracy of ⅟₅₀ inch (0.5 mm). More than 10,000 drawings were produced by the contractors to complete the one million square feet (93,000 m²) of cladding.

▷ **The steelwork** was assembled, sprayed, wrapped, or clad at different points up the building simultaneously. In June 1984, this mast had been "turkey-wrapped" (right) to the first setback at level 30 and had had its cladding panels installed to level 22.

△ *Bamboo scaffolding is used in Asia. It is strong yet flexible and lasts for years. Although the traditional raffia that ties the structure together has given way to nylon, the bamboo itself remains popular. As Foster himself remarked, "bamboo scaffold erupts everywhere in Hong Kong. I don't think it would have been possible to build the Bank without it. It goes up faster and more cheaply than western scaffolds, and can resist hurricanes."*

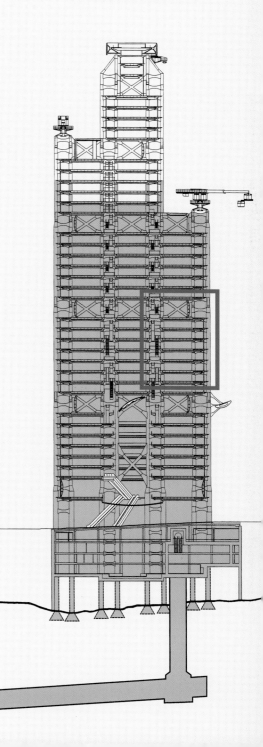

MARCH 1984

STEEL SUPERSTRUCTURE
Steelwork complete to level 33; floor beams installed to level 31 and escape staircases to level 28.

PROTECTION AND CLADDING
On-site spraying complete to level 29; "turkey wrap" to level 8 and cladding to level 3.

SERVICES
Modules fitted to level 22 and subfloor ductwork complete to level 3. First escalators arrive on site.

FITTING OUT
Raised floor and partition installation begins.

BASEMENTS
Floor slab of basement level B3 complete. Chillers installed in level B2; pipework for refrigeration and heat pumps complete.

SEAWATER TUNNEL
Concrete lining added to tunnel.

△ **Most rest periods** *would find workmen snatching some sleep in rather unlikely spots around the site. The deadline for handing over the first section of the building to the Bank, 1 July 1985, was creeping up, and work continued 24 hours a day.*

△ **Balancing at dizzy heights,** *a worker gently guides a steel hanger into position. It was customary in Hong Kong to use local Chinese labor to erect steelwork, a practice that worked well on this project.*

◁ *Silhouetted against the early evening sky and hills of Kowloon, the fifth and final truss is in position at level 41/42. By this time—early June—the main steelwork was substantially complete. All that remained was the assembly of the special top structure, the executive suites, and the viewing gallery.*

◁ *Notched plates provided a fairly accurate method of aligning each "Christmas tree" mast section as it was lowered into position. Each section, usually two stories high and weighing around 46 tons, had to be fitted to an accuracy of less than 1½ inches (40 mm). Long bolts fitted through the plates held the roughly positioned components together. Steelwork was lifted into position at night, but easing it into its final position and welding it took place during the day.*

◁ *A vierendeel beam is maneuvered into position ready to be attached to a mast column. Although the skyscraper was built in just 20 months, using some 27,000 tons of steel, the whole structure was only ⁷⁄₁₆ inch (11 mm) out of alignment over the full height of 586 feet (179 m)—a remarkable degree of accuracy.*

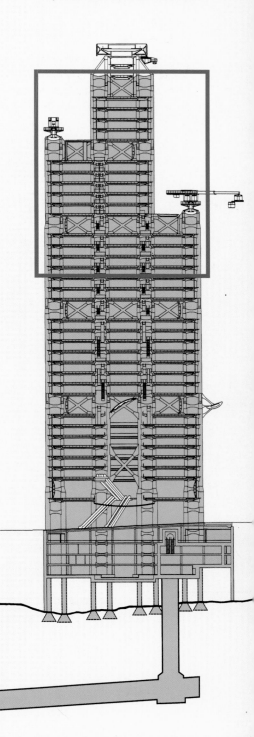

JUNE 1984

STEEL SUPERSTRUCTURE
Complete to fifth truss at level 41/42.

PROTECTION AND CLADDING
External cladding in place to level 22. Glazing of atrium begins.

SERVICES
Modules installed to level 35. All escalators fitted between levels 10 and 35.

FITTING OUT
Raised floor and partitions complete to level 8; suspended ceilings complete with sprinklers and smoke detectors to level 3.

BASEMENTS
Main heat pumps and waste compactors installed. Service yard ready in basement level B3.

SEAWATER TUNNEL
Pipelines installed and fitted to chillers.

◁ **A five-ton elevator** is hoisted into one of the glass-sided elevator shafts of the atrium (left). Once the cars had been installed, their protective plywood panels were replaced with translucent white "shoji" glass, which makes the elevators look like "cubes of light" as they move. The well (above), at the "Cathedral Wall" end of the atrium, is enclosed by a glazed elevator shaft, the bridges that connect the two sides of the atrium, and the staircase that links them.

▽ **The underfloor services** of the main banking hall on level 3 are now complete and ready for inspection. A space 23½ inches (600 mm) deep contains all the air-conditioning, electrical, and telecommunication services as well as the sprinkler pipework for the floor below. Regular outlet points in the raised floor allow maximum flexibility of office layouts.

DECEMBER 1984

STEEL SUPERSTRUCTURE
All steelwork complete except roof canopy.

PROTECTION AND CLADDING
External cladding complete to level 41. Glazing and sunshades fitted to level 36. Installation of internal cladding begins.

SERVICES
All modules and escalators installed. First non-passenger elevators installed in basements.

FITTING OUT
Raised floors and partitions complete to level 16. Suspended ceilings complete to level 10.

BASEMENTS
Installation of generator and transformers complete. Machinery being tested.

SEAWATER TUNNEL
Final tests being carried out.

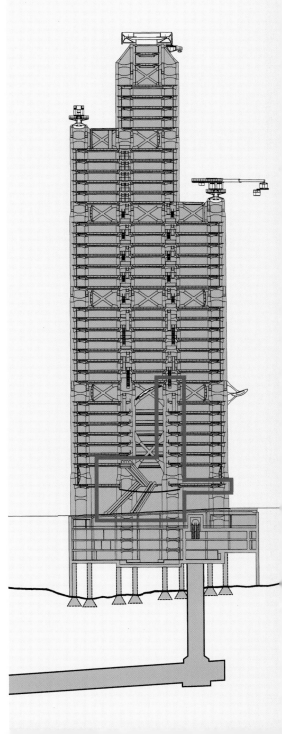

◁ *Escalators were constructed to sweep people up from the plaza through the glazed underbelly to the main banking hall on level 3. When finished, in the fall of 1984, they had the longest unsupported span of any escalators in the world. A special* feng shui *blessing ceremony was held since their position in the building had been so important to the geomancer.*

▽ **The top of the building** is beginning to take shape (below). The final cladding and glazing panels are being installed, and the fittings to mount the signage are now in place. The proximity to the airport meant that no flashing lights or moving signs were permitted, so gray panels with a simple logo were used.

When finished, the executive reception suite (right) included space for small functions, a viewing gallery, and a terrace garden. Although planning regulations forbade the intended use of the top of the building as a helipad, it could easily be converted should restrictions be relaxed.

◁ *Permanent lights illuminate* the first section, from the plaza to level 11 and the first two basements, which was handed over to the Bank on 1 July. Temporary lights above allow work to continue on the rest of the fitting out. Only one red construction crane is left, and the first gray-clad maintenance crane is in position on top of the mast at level 37. Far below, in the plaza, the two bronze lions guard the entrance.

▷ *A double panel* of full-height clear glass was used for the skin of as much of the building as possible. The aluminum mullions, or bars that hold the glass, are suspended from steelwork that also supports the finely detailed sunshade brackets. Angled blades on each of the 4,000 sunshades reduce the amount of direct sunlight entering the floor below without obstructing the view of those on the floor above. They also act as platforms for maintenance and window cleaning.

△ *Four years after their removal* from the front of the old building, the bronze lions, symbols of prosperity for both the Bank and the colony, were moved from their temporary home in Statue Square to their new position at the plaza entrance. At 4 A.M. on 1 June 1985, the most propitious time to move them, geomancer Koo Pak Ling made sure that everything went according to plan. The lions, nicknamed "Stephen" and "Stitt" for former managers, were formally welcomed to their new spot in a ceremony the following week.

MAY–JULY 1985

STEEL SUPERSTRUCTURE
Steelwork finished, roof canopy nearing completion, and first maintenance crane in position.

PROTECTION AND CLADDING
External cladding and glazing completed on 20 May with "topping out" ceremony.

SERVICES
Elevator motor towers in place and 50 percent of elevator cars installed.

FITTING OUT
Subfloor services, raised floors, and partitions complete. Suspended ceilings installed to level 36. First furniture arrives. Internal sunscoop fitted at level 11/12.

BASEMENTS
Chillers and heat pumps operating.

SEAWATER TUNNEL
Completed 1 March 1985.

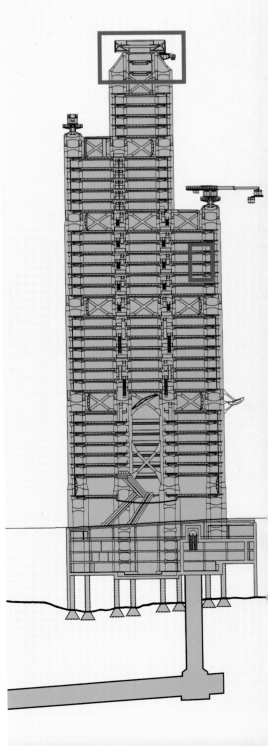

△ **Foster's original sketch** of the sunscoop shows how light would be collected on the outside of the building, reflected inside, and then projected down into the atrium. Foster had wanted light to reach down below the plaza. This idea had to be abandoned, however, because of problems in obtaining suitable glass for the lobby. The computer drawing (above right) shows the final plan.

△ **Most of the 480 individually controlled mirrors** of the external sunscoop were manufactured, assembled, and tested at a factory in Germany. The whole sunscoop was then dismantled and shipped to Hong Kong to be reassembled on site.

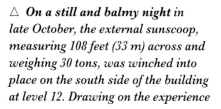

△ **On a still and balmy night** in late October, the external sunscoop, measuring 108 feet (33 m) across and weighing 30 tons, was winched into place on the south side of the building at level 12. Drawing on the experience of solar power stations, the sunscoop is controlled by a sophisticated computer that tracks the sun's height in the sky. Electric motors adjust the mirrors to ensure that they are kept at the best possible angle for light gathering.

▷ **The internal reflectors,** which are suspended from the ceiling of the atrium, send ripples of early morning sunlight into the atrium and down through the glazed underbelly to the plaza. Spotlights fitted between the reflectors not only supplement the variable levels of sunlight reflected in from outside, but also illuminate the atrium at night.

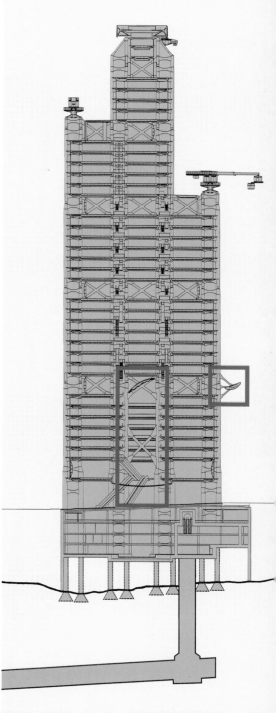

OCTOBER 1985

STEEL SUPERSTRUCTURE
Complete with external sunscoop in place.

PROTECTION AND CLADDING
All complete including external sunscoop.

ROOF CANOPY
Signage panels installed; all suites fully fitted out.

BANKING HALL
Opened for business 20 July.

On 17 November 1985 the completion certificate was presented by Sir Norman Foster and Partners to representatives of the Bank, who formally took possession of their new headquarters building.

△ **The Gothic loftiness** of the atrium preserves the calm atmosphere of the building despite the bustle of the main banking hall at level 3 and the stream of people going up and down the glass-sided escalators that link the inside of the building to the ground floor plaza (right). The main banking hall, which is an acre (4,000 m²) in size, can handle as many as 10,000 transactions each day—many banks only handle that number in a year.

◁ **The official opening ceremony** of the new building took place on 7 April 1986. On the red-carpeted dais erected in the plaza, the Governor of Hong Kong and the Chairman of the Bank declared the Bank open in the presence of nearly 2,500 people. One giant screen relayed the ceremony to people on the banking floors above, while, at two racecourses, more screens allowed 20,000 of the Bank's staff and their families to share the festivities. The entertainment included pipe bands and a magnificent Chinese dragon operated by 44 men.

▷ **The distinctive banding of color,** caused by
the different light sources used in the office floors
and the double-height truss zones, accentuates
the structural components of the building at night.
Each floor was designed with enclosed offices in
the center, near the escalators, and with the outer
third of each floor open plan, with only low
partitions, to allow as many people as possible
to enjoy the magnificent views.

"Whenever you finish a project you always want a second bite at it. You know yourself whether you took advantage of the opportunity to be creative or just let it slip through your fingers. In the case of the Bank, I can honestly say we made the best of the opportunity."

NORMAN FOSTER

INDEX

Numbers in *italics* refer to captions. Individual skyscrapers are indexed under the name of the building and its location.

BIBLIOGRAPHY AND ACKNOWLEDGMENTS

Selected bibliography

Beedle, Lynn S. (ed.) and **Council of Tall Buildings and Urban Habitat** *Second Century of the Skyscraper* Van Nostrand Reinhold, New York, 1988

Breeze, Carla *New York Deco* Rizzoli International Publications, New York, 1993

Condit, Carl W. *The Chicago School of Architecture: A History of Commercial and Public Building in the Chicago Area, 1875–1925* University of Chicago Press, Chicago and London, 1964

Goldberger, Paul *The Skyscraper* Alfred A. Knopf, Inc., New York, 1981; Allen Lane, London, 1982

Harper, Tim (ed.) *Insight CityGuides: Chicago* APA Publications (HK) Ltd, Hong Kong, 1991

Huxtable, Ada Louise *The Tall Building Artistically Reconsidered: The Search for a Skyscraper Style* University of California Press, Berkeley, Los Angeles and Oxford, 1992

Lambot, Ian (ed.) *The Construction: The New Headquarters for the Hongkong and Shanghai Banking Corporation* Ian Lambot, Hong Kong, 1985

——*Norman Foster, Foster Associates: Buildings and Projects Volume 3 1978–1985* Watermark Publications, Hong Kong, 1989

Maitland, Derek *The Insider's Guide to Hong Kong* Merehurst Press, London, 1987

Saliga, Pauline A. (ed.) *Fragments of Chicago's Past: The Collection of Architectural Fragments at The Art Institute of Chicago* The Art Institute of Chicago, Chicago, 1990

——*The Sky's the Limit: A Century of Chicago Skyscrapers* Rizzoli International Publications, New York, 1990

Scuri, Piera *Late-Twentieth-Century Skyscrapers* Van Nostrand Reinhold, New York, 1990

Sharp, Dennis (ed.) *The Illustrated Dictionary of Architects and Architecture* Headline Book Publishing, London, 1991

Williams, Stephanie *Hongkong Bank: The Building of Norman Foster's Masterpiece* Jonathan Cape, London, 1989

Zenfell, Martha *Insight CityGuides: New York City* APA Publications (HK) Ltd, Hong Kong, 1991

Acknowledgments

Marshall Editions would like to thank the following people for their assistance in compiling this book:

The John Buck Company for allowing the author and photographer to explore the Sears Tower.

Hal Iyengar and Karla Kaulfuss at Skidmore, Owings & Merrill for their help in producing the artworks on pages 24–25 and 42–45.

John Albright at DeStefano and Partners Architects in Chicago for his assistance with the artwork on pages 24–25.

Sir Norman Foster and Partners for their help with chapter three.

Copy editors: Isabella Raeburn, Maggi McCormick
Editorial director: Sophie Collins
Managing editor: Lindsay McTeague
Production editor: Sorrel Everton
DTP editor: Pennie Jelliff
Index: Christine Shuttleworth
Research: Liz Ferguson, Simon Beecroft
Art assistant: Eileen Batterberry
Production: Sarah Hinks

Printed in EU Officine Grafiche De Agostini - Novara 1995
Bound by Legatoria del Verbano S.p.A.